Preface

MURDER, SHE WROTE, starring Angela Lansbury, ran on television for a remarkable twelve seasons. It was the highest-rated drama series on television for nine consecutive seasons, and over ten billion viewers tuned in to guess who done it before sweet Jessica Fletcher did. During that long run, the stars, staffers, and gaffers became like family to each other, and the weekly viewers came to feel like friends. Everybody involved in creating the show, as well as their audience, was sad to see the last mystery unraveled.

This delightful cookbook from the cast and crew of *Murder, She Wrote* is a wonderful memento for all those who loved the show and enjoy good eating. It seemed that everyone who worked on the set shared a passion for food. On shooting breaks and between big scene changes, many of us would gather around the craft services table, which served terrific food all day long, and swap recipes and stories of entertaining. Food even worked its way into the script, as Jessica Fletcher loved dining out and was often found snooping for clues at a dinner party or discussing a case over lunch. One day during a shooting break, it struck me that the cast and crew could easily create a cookbook together. Two minutes later Angela Lansbury came walking up, and when I asked her about it, she said, "Start collecting!" The result: 350 recipes as diverse as the people who contributed them, from homespun classics like chicken and dumplings or Cabot Cove spicy seafood chowder to ethnic delicacies like South African potjie, Irish soda bread, and Moroccan curried eggplant. As an extra treat, we added a chapter that describes who does what behind the scenes on a show, and what it takes to put a successful series together.

The set of *Murder, She Wrote* was a unique place to work in Hollywood. Angela Lansbury's warm personal style created a family atmosphere for the cast and crew, and during her seven years as executive producer, she made the show special by hiring outstanding actors she had worked with in the past. It was typical of her to want to donate all the profits of this cookbook to a favorite charity, "Aid for AIDS," which benefits men, women, and children afflicted with AIDS by providing financial assistance for basic necessities like housing, utilities, health insurance premiums, and medications.

We hope all our loyal viewers will enjoy using our cookbook as much as we enjoyed putting it together. Thanks, everybody!

Tom Culver and Nancy Goodman Iland

The

MURDER, SHE WROTE

Cookbook

Tom Culver and Nancy Goodman Iland

CHICAGO
REVIEW
PRESS

Library of Congress Cataloging-in-Publication Data

The Murder She Wrote Cookbook: recipes from cast and crew / edited by Tom Culver and Nancy Goodman Iland.
cm.

Includes index
ISBN 1-55652-316-5
1. Cookery. 2. Murder, She Wrote (Television program)
I. Culver, Tom 1939- . II. Iland, Nancy Goodman, 1960- .
TX714.M863 1997 641.5—dc21 97-5961
CIP

© Tom Culver and Nancy Goodman Iland
All Rights Reserved
Published by Chicago Review Press, Incorporated
814 North Franklin Street
Chicago, Illinois 60610
ISBN 1-55652-316-5
Printed in the United States of America
5 4 3 2 1

Acknowledgments

We would like to give special thanks to MCA/Universal for allowing us to use the *Murder, She Wrote* name and logo. Also many thanks to Angela Lansbury for her enthusiasm and graciousness toward this project. We want to thank Linda M. Bell for her typing; Ken Beyer for pulling the original cookbook together; Hub Braden for his tireless efforts on the project; John Carranza for designing the beautiful book cover on the original edition; Dana Crocker, who took care of all our transportation needs; Susan Vercelli for all her hard work in coordinating this book; Katheryn Wallace, executive assistant to Ms. Lansbury, for smoothing out all the wrinkles; and Toby Iland for all his love and support. Most of all we wish to thank the cast and crew for their wonderful recipes.

Contents

ONE

Appetizers

"Angela Lansbury is so easygoing and personable on the show that one can sometimes forget what an enormous star she is. One day, she and I and another actor were all standing in a row assuming rather odd positions, in order to accommodate a director who was lining up a fancy camera angle. We knew the shot was going to look good, but we still felt a little silly doing it. I commented that we must look as crazy as the three characters in The Mad Woman of Chaillot. The other actor countered with, 'They ought to make a musical out of that.' And Angela blithely added, 'They did. It was called Dear World.' And we all realized, with a gasp, that she had starred in it! On Broadway! Who else in the world would have a career so large and varied that the merest joke could end up referring to it?"

—Bruce Gray, actor

Artichoke Appetizers

BOB WILLIAMS, FIRST ASSISTANT DIRECTOR

*2 jars (6 ounces each) marinated
  artichoke hearts
1 small yellow onion, chopped
1 clove garlic, minced
4 large eggs, beaten
⅓ cup fine dry breadcrumbs
¼ teaspoon salt
Black pepper to taste
Dried oregano to taste
Tabasco sauce to taste
½ pound sharp Cheddar cheese,
  shredded
2 tablespoons minced parsley*

Preheat the oven to 325°F. Drain the juice from 1 jar of artichokes into a skillet and heat over high heat. Drain and discard the juice from the other jar. Chop the artichokes from both jars and set aside. Add the onion and garlic to the skillet and sauté until the onion is translucent. In a medium bowl, mix the eggs, breadcrumbs, salt, pepper, oregano, and Tabasco sauce. Stir in the cheese, parsley, chopped artichokes, and sautéed onions and garlic and mix well. Pour into an 8-inch square greased baking dish. Bake for ½ hour or until set. Let cool in pan. Serve warm or cold, cut into 1-inch squares.

Makes about 32 servings

Shrimp and Cocktail Sauce

JENNIFER WARREN, ACTRESS

*1 yellow onion, diced
Juice of 1 lemon
1 teaspoon ketchup
1 cup plain nonfat yogurt
1 teaspoon red or white wine
  vinegar
1 tablespoon sour cream
1 pound jumbo shrimp, in shells*

In a serving bowl, combine the onion, lemon juice, ketchup, yogurt, vinegar, and sour cream. Boil the shrimp in salted water briefly until they turn pink. Remove and drain. Serve the shrimp in the shell with the sauce on the side for dipping.

Makes 8 servings

Mock Shrimp Cocktail

TOMMY MARGOZEWITZ, PROP MAN

1 can (10¾ ounces) tomato soup,
  undiluted
16 ounces cream cheese, softened
1½ tablespoons unflavored gelatin,
  softened in ½ cup cold water
¾ cup chopped celery
¾ cup chopped scallions
1 cup mayonnaise
20 ounces canned small deveined
  shrimp

In a small saucepan, bring the tomato soup to a boil. Add the cream cheese and beat until smooth. Add the gelatin and let cool, then stir in the celery, scallions, and mayonnaise. Chill in the refrigerator until thickened about 1 hour. Gently stir in the shrimp. Serve chilled with assorted crackers.

Makes 8 servings

Cheese Balls

RUTH ANN MUSBACH, ATMOSPHERE

8 ounces cream cheese, softened
2 cups shredded sharp Cheddar
  cheese
1 teaspoon lemon juice
2 tablespoons Worcestershire sauce
1 tablespoon minced pimientos
1 tablespoon minced green bell
  pepper
1 tablespoon minced yellow onion
Salt and black pepper to taste
¼ cup pecan pieces

Mix the cream cheese and Cheddar cheese together in a blender or food processor until smooth. Add the lemon juice and Worcestershire sauce. By hand, blend in the pimientos, green peppers, and onion. Season lightly with salt and pepper. Roll this mixture into 1 large or 2 smaller balls. Roll the balls in the pecan pieces. Wrap in plastic wrap and chill until firm, about 2 hours.

Makes 1 large or 2 small cheese balls: 8 to 10 servings

Chicken Liver Pâté

LINDA PURL, ACTRESS

1 pound chicken livers
½ medium yellow onion, chopped
¼ pound (1 stick) butter
1 clove garlic, minced
½ teaspoon dried tarragon
½ teaspoon sesame seeds
¼ teaspoon dried thyme
¼ teaspoon salt
¼ teaspoon ground nutmeg
¼ teaspoon ground cinnamon
Chopped fresh parsley to garnish

Rinse the chicken livers in cold water and drain on paper towels. Remove and discard any membrane or fat. Chop and set aside. In a large skillet, sauté the onion in the butter until lightly browned. Add the chicken livers and remaining ingredients. Cook until the chicken livers are firm and pink in the center, about 10 minutes. Do not overcook. Pour the mixture into a food processor and blend until smooth. Place in a lightly greased 2-cup mold or bowl and chill until firm. Turn out onto a serving platter and garnish with fresh parsley. Serve with crackers or toast.

Makes 8 servings

Italian Lemon Chicken Thighs

FRAN BENNETT, ACTRESS

6 cloves garlic, minced
2 tablespoons fresh rosemary
¼ teaspoon curry powder
¼ teaspoon ground ginger
¼ teaspoon ground cumin
¼ teaspoon ground coriander
⅓ cup wine or dry vermouth
½ cup fresh lemon juice

In a large mixing bowl, combine the garlic, rosemary, curry powder, ginger, cumin, coriander, wine or vermouth, lemon juice, and salt. Season with pepper and mix well. Add the chicken pieces to the bowl, stir to coat well, cover, and marinate overnight or at least 2 hours. Preheat the oven to 350°F. Remove the chicken pieces from the marinade and

Salt to taste

Coarsely ground black pepper to taste

20 chicken thighs, skin removed

place in a large baking dish lightly greased with olive oil. Pour enough marinade over the thighs to cover the bottom of the dish, to a depth of about ¼ inch. Bake for 20 minutes on each side. Serve hot, cold, or room temperature.

Makes about 20 servings

Chicken Long Rice

TAMLYN TOMITA, ACTRESS

5 pounds chicken thighs, skin removed

12 cups water

2 tablespoons freshly grated ginger (about a 2-inch piece)

2 tablespoons Hawaiian rock salt (found in Asian food markets) or substitute regular salt

2 cloves garlic, minced

20 ounces long rice Saifun bean threads (found in the Asian food section of most markets)

4 scallions, sliced

5 cups hot, cooked rice

In a large saucepan, cover the chicken with 12 cups of water. Add the ginger, 1 tablespoon of the rock salt, add the garlic and simmer for 45 minutes or until tender. Let cool and reserve the broth. Bone the chicken and cut into bite-size pieces. Remove the ginger and discard. Add the long rice to the reserved broth and let stand for ½ hour. Remove the long rice and cut into 4-inch lengths. Return the long rice to the broth. Add the scallions (reserving some for garnish), remaining 1 tablespoon rock salt, and chicken. Bring to a boil and simmer for 15 to 20 minutes. Serve over steaming hot rice, using the broth as a sauce. Garnish with the reserved scallions and serve at your next luau. This dish can easily be halved and served as a main meal.

Makes 20 servings

Cocktail Meatballs

CAROLE CHRISTOPHER, SET DRESSER

1 pound ground beef
½ pound pork sausage
2 large eggs
⅔ cup dry breadcrumbs
1 teaspoon dried sage
Salt and black pepper to taste
2 cups ketchup
4 tablespoons cider or red wine
  vinegar
8 tablespoons light or dark brown
  sugar
4 tablespoons soy sauce

Preheat the oven to 325°F. In a large bowl, mix together the beef, sausage, eggs, breadcrumbs, and sage. Season with salt and pepper and form into bite-size balls. Brown in an ungreased skillet. When browned, remove the meatballs to a casserole dish. In a small bowl, mix together the ketchup, vinegar, brown sugar, and soy sauce. Pour the sauce over the meatballs and bake for ½ hour.

Makes 24 meatballs, about 12 servings

Sweet-and-Sour Meatballs

KATHRYN CRESSIDA, ACTRESS

1 can (16 ounces) cranberry sauce
1 can (10¾ ounces) tomato soup,
  undiluted
½ cup water
2 pounds ground beef
½ cup dry breadcrumbs
½ teaspoon salt
½ cup ketchup

Combine the cranberry sauce, soup, and water in a medium saucepan and bring to a simmer. When the mixture bubbles, reduce the heat to low. In a mixing bowl, combine the ground beef, breadcrumbs, salt, and ketchup and mix gently. Form into 2-inch balls and drop into the sauce. Cover and cook for 1½ hours over low heat.

Makes 24 meatballs, about 12 servings

Cheese Puffs

NANCY GOODMAN ILAND, FOODSTYLIST

½ pound Cheddar cheese, shredded
½ cup grated Parmesan cheese
4 scallions, chopped
½ cup mayonnaise

*P*reheat the broiler. Mix all the ingredients together in a blender or food processor. Spread on crackers or toast rounds. Broil until brown on top, about 5 minutes.

Makes 36 cheese puffs, about 18 servings

Hummus

PHIL SHOFNER, PROP MAN

1 pound cooked garbanzo beans
2 to 4 cloves garlic, minced
¼ cup tahini
Salt to taste
1 tablespoon olive oil
Cayenne pepper to taste (optional)

*I*n a food processor or blender, combine all the ingredients and blend until smooth. Serve with pita bread or chips.

Makes 6 servings

Stuffed Mushrooms

KATHERINE CANNON, ACTRESS

12 large mushrooms
1 large clove garlic, minced
1 tablespoon olive oil or safflower
  margarine
½ cup chopped scallions
⅓ cup chopped salted cashews
3 ounces cream cheese, softened
Poultry seasoning to taste
½ cup fine seasoned breadcrumbs

*P*reheat the oven to 450°F. Remove the stems from the mushroom caps and dice the stems. Lightly sauté the mushroom caps and garlic in the olive oil, for 3 to 5 minutes. Remove the caps and set aside. In the same pan, sauté the diced mushroom stems, scallions, and cashews. Blend this mixture with the cream cheese, poultry seasoning, and breadcrumbs. Stuff the mushrooms caps with the mixture, place in a shallow baking pan, and bake for 15 minutes.

Makes 12 stuffed mushrooms, about 6 servings

Spinach Balls

JOHN ARNDT, STAND-IN

6 large eggs, lightly beaten
2 medium yellow onions, chopped
2 packages (10 ounces each)
  frozen chopped spinach, thawed
  and well drained
¾ pound (3 sticks) butter, melted
1 tablespoon Accent seasoning
½ teaspoon dried thyme
2 teaspoons black pepper
1 teaspoon garlic salt

*M*ix the eggs, onions, spinach, butter, Accent, thyme, pepper, and garlic salt together in a medium bowl. Stir in the stuffing mix and Parmesan and chill in the refrigerator for 1 hour. Preheat the oven to 350°F. Roll the

12 ounces instant bread stuffing mix, dry (reserve vegetable mix if included)
½ cup grated Parmesan cheese

mixture into 1-inch balls. Bake on a cookie sheet for 20 minutes. These appetizers can be made in advance, frozen, and reheated.

Makes 75 spinach balls, about 38 servings

Spinach-Stuffed Mushrooms

WILLIE GOMEZ OF BRUCE'S CATERING, PROP FOOD SUPPLIER

50 large mushrooms
5 cloves garlic, crushed
2 tablespoons olive oil
2 tablespoons lemon juice
2 pounds fresh spinach, chopped
½ cup grated Parmesan cheese
¼ teaspoon salt
¼ teaspoon black pepper

$\mathcal{P}$reheat the oven to 350°F. Remove the stems from the mushroom caps and chop the stems into small pieces. Sauté the caps and garlic in the olive oil and 1 table-spoon of the lemon juice for 4 minutes. Remove the mushroom caps and set aside. Blend the chopped stems, spinach, the remaining 1 tablespoon lemon juice, Parmesan, salt, and pepper in a food processor or blender until smooth. Stuff the caps with the mixture and place on an ungreased cookie sheet. Bake for 20 minutes.

Makes 50 stuffed mushrooms, about 25 servings

Salpicon Appetizers

KEVIN CORCORAN, FIRST ASSISTANT DIRECTOR

1 pound flank steak

1 teaspoon salt

1 bunch cilantro, chopped (about ½ cup)

4 medium tomatoes, cored and diced

1 bunch scallions, diced

1 can (4 ounces) diced green chilies

1 tablespoon olive oil

1 cup shredded Monterey Jack cheese

1 large avocado, peeled, seeded, and diced

Juice of ½ lemon or lime

Place the steak in a large pan and cover with water and salt. Simmer for 1 hour. Remove the steak from the pan and allow to cool. Cut into 1-inch strips and shred. In a large serving bowl, toss the shredded steak with the cilantro, tomatoes, scallions, chilies, olive oil, and cheese. Squeeze the lemon or lime juice over the avocado to keep it from being discolored and mix in just before serving. Serve with large tortilla chips. This dish works best if made ahead of time to allow the flavors to blend.

Makes 10 to 12 servings

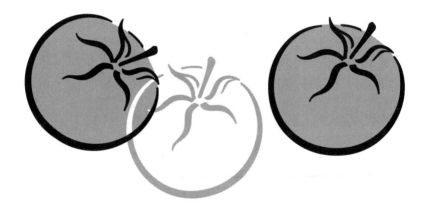

Monterey Quesadillas

ED GRADY, CRAFT SERVICES

1½ cups shredded Monterey Jack
cheese
½ cup shredded Cheddar cheese
1 can (7 ounces) whole mild
green chilies
8 slices cooked ham, chopped
(optional)
½ cup crumbled cooked bacon
(optional)
8 (12-inch) flour tortillas

Mix together all the ingredients except the tortillas. Place the tortillas, one at a time, in an oiled or nonstick skillet. Cover half of each tortilla with ⅛ of the cheese mixture. Fold the other half of the tortilla over and fry on both sides until cheese is melted. Remove, slice into triangles, and serve warm with sour cream, salsa, and guacamole on the side.

Makes about 12 servings

Idaho Wings

STEVE NICKLE, TRANSPORTATION

1 envelope (1½ ounces)
Campbell's Onion Soup &
Recipe Mix
½ cup molasses
½ cup hot picante sauce
½ cup fresh lemon juice
¼ cup soy sauce
3 teaspoons Tabasco sauce
2 pounds chicken wings or drum-
mettes

In a large bowl, combine all the ingredients except the chicken and mix well. Add the chicken and toss well to coat. Cover and chill for 4 hours or overnight. Preheat the oven to 400°F. Place the chicken and marinade in a large baking pan in a single layer. Bake for 45 minutes, basting occasionally.

Makes about 6 servings

Brie and Apple Quesadillas with Mango Salsa

ANDREA MARKS HOLTZMAN OF BRUCE'S CATERING, PROP FOOD SUPPLIER

2 mangoes, peeled and diced
¼ cup coarsely chopped cilantro
¼ cup diced red bell pepper
1 tablespoon finely minced scallion
1 tablespoon white wine vinegar
10 ounces Brie cheese, softened
20 (8-inch) flour tortillas
4 Fuji apples, cored and thinly
  sliced

Combine the mangoes, cilantro, red pepper, scallion, and vinegar. Set aside. Spread the soft Brie over half the flour tortillas. Cover each with thin slices of apple and top with a plain tortilla. Fry the tortillas on both sides until the cheese melts. Cut the tortillas into sixths and top each with a dab of the mango salsa and serve.

Makes 30 servings

TWO

Dips and Spreads

"While I had the pleasure of acting in three episodes of Murder, She Wrote, *the first one was most memorable. One day during our lunch break, my costar and I hijacked a studio golf cart and persuaded the costume designer to sneak away with us for a joyride. And what a joyride it was! We blasted through sets, glided by sound stages, and felt like movie stars. We were merrily cruising around the back lot when we spotted the Universal Studios Tour tram. One wrong turn and the tram was chasing us. We were riding ahead on the tram's route, tripping switches and setting off special effects! We made it rain in Mexico and started an avalanche. When Jaws popped out of the Cabot Cove lagoon, we knew it was time to get back to work. We slid back onto Stage 25 and tried to keep straight faces as the camera started rolling.*"

—*Robb Curtis-Brown, actor*

Curried Cauliflower

MAUREEN O'HERON, WARDROBE

1 head cauliflower (1 pound)
1 cup mayonnaise
1 cup plain yogurt
1 medium or small white onion,
  finely minced
2 cloves garlic, pressed
2 tablespoons curry powder
Salt and black pepper to taste

*C*ut the bottom of the cauliflower so it lays flat. Steam lightly until very soft, then let cool. Mix the remaining ingredients together and pour over the cauliflower. Chill. The cauliflower will be soft enough to spread, so serve with an assortment of crackers. This is best if made the day before so the flavors have a chance to blend.

Makes about 12 servings

Mexican Artichoke Cheese Dip

MARIO ZAVALA, SECOND ASSISTANT CAMERA

1 cup mayonnaise
½ cup sour cream
1 can (7 ounces) diced green
  chilies
1 can (14¾ ounces) artichoke
  hearts, drained and chopped
1 cup grated Parmesan cheese

*P*reheat the oven to 350°F. Mix the mayonnaise, sour cream, chilies, and artichoke hearts together in a casserole dish. Bake for 20 minutes to ½ hour. Sprinkle the Parmesan over the top and bake for 10 minutes more. For color and variety, add canned black olives or chopped pimientos. Serve warm with crackers or toast rounds.

Makes 3 cups, 8 to 10 servings

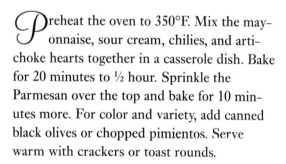

Avocado Crab Dip

PHIL BEESON, UTILITY SOUND TECHNICIAN

1 large avocado, peeled, seeded,
  and cubed
1 tablespoon lemon juice
1 yellow onion, thinly sliced
1 teaspoon Worcestershire sauce
8 ounces cream cheese, softened
¼ cup sour cream
¼ teaspoon salt
1 cup shredded crabmeat

*B*lend the avocado, lemon juice, onion, and Worcestershire sauce in a blender or food processor until smooth. Add the cream cheese, sour cream and salt, and blend until well mixed. Gently stir in the crabmeat. Chill. Serve with potato chips or crackers.

Makes 2 cups, 4 to 6 servings

Layered Mexican Bean Dip

RON MASAK, ACTOR

1 can (8 ounces) refried beans
2 cups sour cream
½ cup picante sauce
2 cups shredded Cheddar cheese
1 large tomato, cored and diced
1 can (7 ounces) sliced black
  olives, drained
3 scallions, chopped (optional)

*S*pread the refried beans to cover the bottom of a large, shallow dish. Layer the sour cream over the beans and pour the picante sauce over the sour cream. Sprinkle the cheese, tomato, olives, and scallions on top. Serve immediately with tortilla chips or corn chips.

Makes 2½ cups, about 8 servings

Chili Dip

JOANIE FRASCO, STAND-IN

1 can (15 ounces) chili without beans
1 can (7 ounces) green chili salsa
1 can (7 ounces) sliced black olives, drained
8 ounces cream cheese
1 tablespoon chili powder
1 cup shredded sharp Cheddar cheese

Mix the chili, salsa, olives, cream cheese, chili powder, and ¾ cup of the Cheddar cheese together in a large skillet. Heat over medium heat until all the cheeses are melted. Spoon into a serving dish and sprinkle the remaining ¼ cup cheese on top. Serve hot with corn chips.

Makes 2½ cups, about 8 servings

Easy Cheese and Salsa Dip

MIKE APPERSON, SECOND COMPANY GRIP

1 pound Velveeta processed cheese, cubed
3 cups salsa, homemade or in a jar

In a microwave-safe bowl, combine the cheese and salsa. Microwave on HIGH for 2 minutes. Stir and cook for an additional 2 minutes, or until desired thickness is achieved. Remove and allow to cool slightly. Stir a few times and serve with tortilla chips.

Makes 2½ cups, about 12 servings

Clam Dip

NANCY GOODMAN ILAND, FOODSTYLIST

8 ounces cream cheese, softened
½ cup sour cream
1 can (6½ ounces) minced clams
1 tablespoon Worcestershire sauce
1 teaspoon grated yellow onion

*M*ix all the ingredients together in a serving bowl and chill. Serve with crackers or French bread.

Makes 2½ cups, about 8 servings

Hot Clam Spread

NANCY GOODMAN ILAND, FOODSTYLIST

2 cans (6½ ounces each) minced
    clams
¼ pound (1 stick) butter, melted
1½ cups cracker crumbs
1 medium yellow onion, chopped
1 tablespoon grated yellow onion
1 tablespoon lemon juice

*P*reheat the oven to 350°F. Drain the juice from 1 can of clams. Mix the drained clams and the other can of clams with juice, with the butter, crumbs, chopped onion, grated onion, and lemon juice. Bake in a shallow dish for ½ hour. Serve immediately spread on crackers or toast.

Makes 2½ cups: about 8 servings

Zingy Clam Dip

GREG LUMTZEL, FIRST ASSISTANT CAMERA

2 cups sour cream
2 cans (6½ ounces each) minced
  clams
2 cans (6½ ounces each) chopped
  clams
1 tablespoon garlic powder
1 tablespoon Worcestershire sauce
1 tablespoon horseradish
Tabasco sauce to taste

*M*ix all the ingredients together in a serving bowl, chill, and serve with crackers.

Makes 2½ cups, about 8 servings

Killer Crab Dip

BARNEY MCNULTY, DIALOGUE SPECIALIST

½ pound Velveeta processed cheese
½ cup mayonnaise
¼ cup sour cream
¼ cup crabmeat

*M*elt the cheese, mayonnaise, and sour cream together in the top of a double boiler. Add the crabmeat and serve warm with assorted crackers.

Makes 1½ cups, about 4 servings

Kickoff Party Dip

BEVERLY SEIFERT, DRIVER TO MS. LANSBURY

32 ounces cream cheese, softened
2 packages (8 ounces each)
 Hidden Valley Ranch Party Dip
1¾ cups diced red bell pepper
1 cup diced green bell pepper
½ cup pitted and diced black olives
1 can (7 ounces) diced green
 chilies

*M*ix all the ingredients together and chill overnight. Serve with crackers, chips, or vegetables.

Makes about 15 servings

Ruth's Spinach Dip

TERESA AUSTIN, MAKEUP ARTIST

1 package (10 ounces) frozen
 chopped spinach
½ cup chopped fresh parsley
½ teaspoon dried dill
Juice of ½ lemon
½ cup chopped scallions
1 cup sour cream
1 cup mayonnaise
Salt and black pepper to taste

*S*team the spinach and drain well. Mix with the remaining ingredients and chill for 24 hours. Serve with crackers or chips.

Makes 2 cups, 8 to 10 servings

Cabot Cove Fisherman's Cocktail Spread

STEPHEN SWOFFORD, ASSOCIATE PRODUCER

8 ounces cream cheese, softened
½ cup sour cream
¼ cup mayonnaise
½ pound fresh bay shrimp, rinsed and drained
1 cup seafood cocktail sauce
2 cups shredded mozzarella cheese
3 scallions, chopped
1 tomato, cored and diced
1 green bell pepper, chopped

Mix the cream cheese, sour cream, and mayonnaise together and spread in a 12-inch dish or pie plate. Scatter the shrimp over the cheese mixture, then top with the cocktail sauce, mozzarella cheese, scallions, tomatoes, and green peppers. Cover and chill until ready to serve. Serve with crackers.

Makes about 8 servings

Taco Dip

JIM WEIS, SECOND ASSISTANT DIRECTOR

1 pound lean ground beef
1 package (1¼ ounces) taco mix
1 can (8 ounces) tomato sauce
1 cup water
1 cup shredded Cheddar cheese (optional)
1 small yellow onion, chopped (optional)

Brown the ground beef in a skillet. Drain off all liquid and place the cooked meat in a serving bowl. Add the taco mix, tomato sauce, and water and mix well. Top with the shredded Cheddar cheese and chopped onion if desired. Serve with tortilla chips.

Makes 2 cups, 8 to 10 servings

Fondue American

PAUL ISLEY, SET DRESSER

1 envelope (1½ ounces) Lipton's Onion Soup Mix
2 cups tomato juice
4 teaspoons lemon juice
1 pound processed American cheese, shredded
1 loaf French or rye bread, cut into 1-inch cubes

*I*n a fondue dish, mix together the soup mix, tomato juice, lemon juice, and cheese. Place over heat, melt, and serve with bread cubes for dipping.

Makes 8 to 10 servings

Crab Fondue

BOB WILLIAMS, FIRST ASSISTANT DIRECTOR

16 ounces cream cheese
2 cloves garlic, minced
½ cup mayonnaise
2 teaspoons yellow mustard
¼ cup dry sherry
1 tablespoon minced yellow onion
Salt to taste
1 can (6½ ounces) crabmeat
1 can (6 ounces) white tuna

*M*ix together the cream cheese, garlic, mayonnaise, mustard, sherry, onion, and salt in a saucepan and cook over low heat. Add the crabmeat and tuna. Mix gently and heat until warmed through. Serve with crackers, potato chips, or raw vegetables.

Makes 25 servings

THREE

Soups

"*My youth as a southern preacher's son prepared me a little for my first role on the show in the episode "Murder in the Electric Cathedral." The script was very good, and although I had a touch of laryngitis, the part of Reverend Willy John Fargo, entrepreneur and soul-saver extraordinaire, was irresistible. While shooting the hospital scene with Angela, I had to stop over and over again to clear my heavenly pipes. Finally, I took a moment to breathe and apologize for the ruined takes. 'It's all right, dear. It happens to the best of us,' said Angela matter-of-factly. This soft comment made with her world-class smile typifies the encompassing warmth of her personal style and her continuing professionalism.*"

—Steve Forrest, actor

Sopa de Albondigas

DOLORES DOMASIN, STAND-IN

1 cup soft bread cubes
¼ cup milk
1 pound lean ground beef
1 large egg
½ teaspoon seasoned salt
1 cup diced celery
⅓ to ½ cup coarsely chopped
  cilantro
1 large yellow onion, minced
½ cup sliced carrots
2 cups cubed zucchini
2½ cups beef broth
1 can (28 ounces) whole tomatoes
1 bay leaf

In a mixing bowl, combine the bread cubes and milk. Mix in the ground beef, egg, and seasoned salt. Chill ½ hour. In a large kettle, combine the celery, cilantro, onion, carrots, zucchini, broth, tomatoes, and bay leaf. Bring to a boil, cover, reduce heat, and simmer for 15 minutes. Shape the meat mixture into 15 or more meatballs. Add the meatballs to the soup. Cover and simmer for another 45 minutes, or until the meatballs are cooked through. Serve immediately.

Makes 8 servings

Autumn Soup

JOHN P. BRUCE, SENIOR SET DESIGNER

1 pound lean ground beef
1 cup chopped yellow onion
4 cups water
1 cup chopped carrots
1 cup diced celery
1½ cups cubed potatoes
2 teaspoons salt
1 teaspoon bottled Brown Bouquet
  sauce

In a large saucepan, brown the ground beef. Drain off the fat. Stir in the onions and cook until the onions are soft. Stir in the water, carrots, celery, potatoes, salt, Brown Bouquet sauce, pepper, bay leaves, and basil. Heat to boiling, then reduce heat, cover, and simmer for 20 minutes. Add the tomatoes. If desired, add a spoonful of cornstarch to thick-

¼ teaspoon black pepper
1 to 2 bay leaves
⅛ teaspoon dried basil
6 fresh tomatoes, chopped or 1 can
(28 ounces) crushed tomatoes,
undrained
Tabasco sauce to taste

en. Add a few drops of Tabasco sauce to taste. Cover and simmer for 10 minutes longer or until vegetables are tender.

Makes 6 servings

Val's Homemade Chicken Soup

VALERIE WILDMAN, ACTRESS

1 whole chicken
1 pound egg noodles
3 celery stalks, chopped
3 carrots, chopped
1 white onion, chopped
1 cup chopped spinach (optional)
1 cup chopped broccoli (optional)
1 cup chopped yellow squash
(optional)
Salt and black pepper to taste

*P*lace the chicken in a large stockpot. Cover with water and boil for 1 hour or until the meat falls away from the bone. Remove the bones and skin, skim and discard the fat, chop the meat into small chunks, and return it to the broth. Add the egg noodles, chopped vegetables, salt, and pepper. Simmer for 10 minutes, or until the vegetables and noodles are tender. The taste of this soup intensifies with age.

Makes 6 servings

Chicken Gumbo

GRETCHEN GERMAN, ACTRESS

STOCK

1 chicken, about 3½ pounds
3 quarts water
2 outer stalks celery with leaves
1 carrot, chopped
1 medium yellow onion, quartered
1 bay leaf
1 teaspoon salt

GUMBO

⅓ cup oil
½ cup flour
1 pound okra, washed and cut in
* ¼-inch pieces*
1 large yellow onion, chopped
¾ cup chopped celery
½ cup chopped green bell pepper
½ cup chopped scallions
3 cloves garlic, minced
½ cup chopped fresh parsley
1 bay leaf
¾ teaspoon dried thyme
½ teaspoon dried marjoram
1 teaspoon dried basil
1 can (16 ounces) whole tomatoes
* with juice*
½ pound ham, cubed
1 pound shrimp, peeled and
* deveined*
1 pound smoked sausage, sliced
* and cooked*
1 tablespoon Worcestershire sauce

Salt and pepper to taste
Cayenne pepper to taste
Tabasco sauce to taste
3 cups hot cooked white rice

*T*o make the stock: In a large stock pot, combine and boil all the stock ingredients. Reduce heat and simmer for 25 minutes, skimming top to remove foam and fat. Remove meat from the bones, chop, and reserve both the meat and the bones. Return the bones to the stock and continue to simmer for 35 minutes.

To make the gumbo: In a large, heavy pot, heat the oil and gradually add flour, stirring constantly until medium brown. Add the okra, onion, celery, and green pepper. Cook, stirring until the okra is no longer stringy. Add the scallions, garlic, parsley, bay leaf, thyme, marjoram, basil, tomatoes with juice, ham, chicken meat from the stock, and the shrimp. Strain the stock and slowly stir into the gumbo. Add the sausage. Add the Worcestershire sauce and season with salt, pepper, cayenne pepper, and Tabasco sauce. Simmer uncovered 1½ hours, stirring occasionally. Serve over rice.

Makes 6 servings

Portuguese Red Bean Soup

OFFICER CLARK, LOCATION POLICE

1 pound dried kidney beans,
   washed, soaked overnight, and
   rinsed
3 meaty ham hocks
2 cloves garlic, minced
1 large yellow onion, sliced
2 stalks celery, sliced
2 large hot Portuguese sausages,
   or 2 large Polish sausages plus 3
   chopped dried hot red peppers,
   cut into 1-inch pieces
1 can (8 ounces) tomato sauce
4 large potatoes, diced
1 small head cabbage, coarsely
   chopped
Salt and black pepper to taste
6 cups hot cooked white rice

*S*immer the kidney beans and ham hocks in 10 cups water until tender, about ½ hour. Remove the ham hocks, discard the bones, and return the meat to the pot. Add the garlic, onion, celery, sausage, and tomato sauce. Simmer for 15 to 20 minutes. Add the potatoes, cabbage, salt, and pepper. Simmer for another 15 to 20 minutes. Serve over white rice.

Makes 12 servings

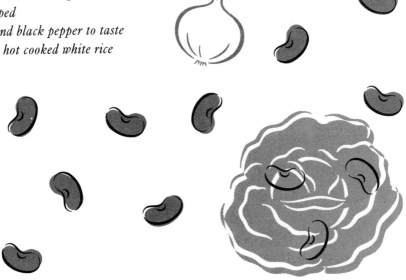

Ten Bean Soup

DAVID SCOTT, PROP MAN

2 cups assorted dried beans
2 cups diced smoked turkey
 sausage
1 medium yellow onion, chopped
3 cloves garlic, minced
1 can (28 ounces) crushed tomatoes
Juice of 1 lemon
Black pepper to taste
¼ teaspoon Tabasco sauce
 (optional)

Rinse the dried beans, place in a large kettle, cover with water, and soak overnight. Rinse and drain again. Add the turkey sausage to the beans. Add 2 quarts water and the onion and garlic. Simmer for 2½ hours. Add tomatoes, lemon juice, pepper, and Tabasco sauce, if desired. Simmer for 45 minutes. Serve with a green salad and Italian or French bread.

Makes 12 servings

Tuscan Vegetable Bean Soup

LISA AKEY AND RAPHAEL SBARGE, ACTORS

5 cloves garlic, minced
2 carrots, minced
1 yellow onion, minced
2 stalks celery, minced
1 cup extra-virgin olive oil
3½ cups chicken stock, homemade
 or canned
2 cups water
3 cups dried beans, any type,
 soaked overnight and rinsed

In a large stockpot, combine the garlic, carrots, onion, celery, and olive oil. Cook over medium heat for 20 minutes, or until the vegetables are golden brown and caramelized. Add the chicken stock, water, beans, tomatoes, Swiss chard leaves, and

4 medium-ripe tomatoes, cored
  and cut into chunks
3 cups torn Swiss chard leaves,
  tough ends discarded
2 cups broccoli florets
Salt and black pepper to taste
Cayenne pepper to taste

broccoli. If desired, you may also add additional chopped carrots, sliced mushrooms, and chopped zucchini. Simmer the soup for 2 to 3 hours. Salt generously and add black pepper and cayenne to taste. This soup improves with age.

Makes 12 servings

Split Pea Soup with Ham

TOM CULVER, WARDROBE

2½ cups dried split peas
1 ham bone with at least 1 cup
  ham on it
3 tablespoons butter
1 yellow onion, chopped
  (approximately 1 cup)
8 cups water
Black pepper to taste

Soak the peas overnight in water and drain. Remove the excess fat from the ham bone. Melt the butter in a stockpot, add the chopped yellow onion and ham bone, and cook, stirring often, for 5 minutes. Add the peas, water, and pepper to taste and simmer for 1 hour, or until the peas are mushy. Remove the ham bone, scrape off the meat, and set aside. Purée the soup in a food processor or blender. Return the soup to the pot and add the ham. Reheat over low heat, stirring frequently, before serving.

Makes 8 servings

Russian Hot Cabbage Soup

VERA YURTCHUK, MAKEUP ARTIST

1 head cabbage, shredded
2 carrots, chopped
1 can (16 ounces) sauerkraut,
 drained and rinsed
1 yellow onion, peeled
1 carrot, scraped
1 potato, peeled
¼ cup any cooking oil except
 olive oil
4 cups water
Pepper to taste

*P*lace all the ingredients in a stock pot. Bring to a boil and simmer, covered, for 2 hours. Remove and discard the onion, carrots, and potato. Stir and serve heated with black bread. Do not serve with sour cream.

Makes 6 servings

Martha's Vineyard Lobster Bisque

SANDY ROTBERG, PRODUCTION

2 small or 1 large fresh lobster
 (about 1½ pounds lobster meat)
½ cup chopped yellow onion
¼ pound (1 stick) butter
1 tablespoon flour
2 cups clam juice
2 tablespoons cornstarch
1 cup lobster tomalley (optional)
½ cup cream sherry
Salt and black pepper to taste

*C*ut the lobster meat into small chunks and sauté with the onion in the butter over medium heat until the onions are translucent, about 7 minutes, while sprinkling in the flour. Do not let the onion brown. In a separate saucepan, heat the clam juice and cornstarch diluted with 3 tablespoons water. Boil for 1 minute. Add the lobster and onion mixture, tomalley, sherry, salt, pepper, and Worcestershire sauce. Simmer for 8 minutes.

Dash of Worcestershire sauce
2 quarts light cream
Chopped fresh parsley to garnish
Paprika to taste

Then add the cream and simmer over a very low flame or in the top of a double boiler for another 3 minutes. Do not boil the cream. Garnish with parsley and sprinkle with paprika.

Makes 10 to 12 servings

Asparagus Soup

BARBARA MCHUGH, COSTUMER

*1 pound fresh asparagus, coarse
  ends removed*
1½ cups chicken broth
*2 tablespoons chopped yellow
  onion*
1 cup milk or cream
Salt and black pepper to taste

Cook the asparagus in 2 cups boiling water until tender. Drain, reserving 1 cup of the water. Cut off the tips to ½ inch and chop them, reserving the stems. Place the chicken broth, onion, and 1 cup reserved water in a pan and bring to a boil. Purée the asparagus stems in a food processor or blender and add to the chicken broth mixture. Reduce the heat to a simmer and stir in the milk or cream. Season with salt and pepper. Before serving, sprinkle the chopped asparagus tips on top.

Makes 4 servings

Spicy Seafood Chowder

KAITLIN HOPKINS, ACTRESS

2 tablespoons olive oil
2 cloves garlic, minced
1 yellow onion, chopped
1 large green bell pepper,
 coarsely chopped
1 fresh jalapeño pepper, seeded
 and chopped
1 teaspoon red pepper flakes
1 cup fish stock
¼ cup dry red wine
2 cans (16 ounces each) whole
 tomatoes, coarsely chopped,
 with juice
2 tablespoons tomato paste
1½ tablespoons sugar
1 teaspoon dried oregano
1 teaspoon dried basil
1 bay leaf
1 baking potato, peeled and cut
 into ½-inch pieces
Salt and freshly ground black
 pepper to taste
12 small clams in the shell,
 well scrubbed
½ pound swordfish or sea bass
 fillets, cut into 2-inch pieces
½ pound raw shrimp, peeled and
 deveined
½ cup chopped cilantro
2 limes, cut into wedges

In a large pot, heat the oil over medium heat. Add the garlic, onion, bell pepper, jalapeño pepper, and pepper flakes and sauté for 2 to 3 minutes, or until the onion is translucent. Add the stock, wine, tomatoes, tomato paste, sugar, oregano, basil, bay leaf, and potato. Bring to a boil, then reduce heat, cover, and simmer, stirring occasionally, for ½ hour, or until the soup is thick but still fairly liquid. Season to taste with salt and pepper. Add the clams, discarding any that are cracked or open. Add the fish and shrimp. Raise the heat slightly, cover, and cook for 7 to 10 minutes until the fish flakes, the shrimp turn pink, and the clams open. Discard any clams that do not open during cooking. Garnish with the cilantro and serve with lime wedges on the side.

Makes 8 servings

Seafood Gazpacho

BRETT PORTER, ACTOR

1 large yellow onion, diced
1 large red onion, diced
1 large cucumber, diced
8 to 10 scallions, diced, leaving
   1 to 2 inches of green
1 large green bell pepper, diced
1 large red bell pepper, diced
1 large celery stalk, diced
1 can (8 ounces) diced water
   chestnuts
1 can (7 ounces) diced green
   chilies
2 large fresh jalapeño peppers,
   diced
4 cloves garlic, finely chopped
1 pound jumbo shrimp without
   tails, cooked
1 pound scallops, cooked
¼ cup chopped cilantro
¼ cup Worcestershire sauce
2 liters Bloody Mary mix
¼ cup lime juice
Salt to taste
Tabasco sauce to taste
Freshly ground black pepper to
   taste
Cayenne pepper to taste
Paprika to taste
½ pint sour cream to garnish

Combine all the ingredients except the sour cream in a large serving bowl, adding the spices and seasonings to taste. Be sure the shrimp and scallops are fully cooked. Let sit for at least 4 hours in the refrigerator. Garnish with sour cream and serve chilled. For a variation, try adding 1 cup vodka, 1 cup vermouth, or 1 cup white wine before refrigerating.

Makes 20 servings

Mushroom Soup and Cream Sauce

ANTHONY SHAW, DIRECTOR

3 tablespoons butter, softened
3 tablespoons flour
1 cup milk, warmed
Salt and black pepper to taste
1 pound fresh mushrooms, finely
  chopped
2 stalks celery, chopped
2 sprigs parsley, chopped
4 small yellow onions, chopped
1 can (14½ ounces) chicken broth

*I*n a small saucepan, mix together the butter and flour. Slowly add the warmed milk to the butter and flour mixture, stirring constantly over low heat. Cook until thick. Season with salt and pepper and set aside. In another saucepan, combine the mushrooms, celery, parsley, onions, and chicken broth and simmer for 20 minutes. Add 1 cup of the butter sauce, stir, and serve.

Makes 2 servings

Mushroom Barley Soup

VERA YURTCHUK, MAKEUP ARTIST

8½ cups beef broth
6 tablespoons barley
1 cup cubed potatoes
1 cup chopped carrots
1 cup chopped yellow onion
1 cup coarsely chopped celery
½ cup green peas
1 cup sliced mushrooms
1 teaspoon chopped fresh parsley
  or dill

*C*ombine the beef broth and barley in a large stockpot and simmer for ½ hour. Add the potatoes, carrots, onion, celery, peas, and mushrooms and simmer for 1 hour more. During the last 15 minutes of cooking, add the parsley or dill.

Makes 6 servings

Polish Mushroom Soup

CAROL LUPO, WARDROBE

7¼ cups chicken broth
7¼ cups beef consommé
7¼ cups water
1 cup pearl barley
1 pound carrots, chopped
1 stalk celery, chopped
1 white onion, chopped
1 leek, white part only, chopped
3 tablespoons butter
½ pound mushrooms, chopped
3 tablespoons cornstarch
Worcestershire sauce to taste
Tabasco sauce to taste

In a 6-quart pot, combine the chicken broth, beef consommé, water, and pearl barley. In a skillet, sauté the carrots, celery, onion, and leek in the butter for 10 minutes. Add the cooked vegetables to the broth mixture. In a separate saucepan, boil the mushrooms for 10 minutes. Pour off the water and add the mushrooms to the soup. Boil for 25 minutes. Dissolve the cornstarch with 4 tablespoons water and add to the soup while boiling. Season with Worcestershire and Tabasco sauces. Serve with buttered French bread.

Makes 12 servings

Hot or Cold Tomato Soup

MARK BURLEY, PRODUCER

1 yellow onion, chopped
2 tablespoons butter
1 baking potato, peeled
  and chopped
2 cloves garlic, minced
10 ripe Roma tomatoes, chopped
Salt and black pepper to taste
Lemon juice to taste
Honey to taste
2 cups vegetable stock
¼ cup plain yogurt
4 sprigs fresh basil
1 cup croutons

In skillet, lightly sauté the onion in the butter until translucent. Add the potato and garlic and stir over low heat. Add the tomatoes, salt, pepper, lemon juice, and honey. Stir in the stock and simmer until all the vegetables are tender. Place the soup in a blender and purée. Serve the soup warm or cold with yogurt, a sprig of basil, and croutons to garnish.

Makes 4 servings

French Onion Soup

SUSAN VERCELLI, PRODUCTION COORDINATOR

2 yellow onions, chopped
4 tablespoons butter
3 cups beef broth
1 box (12 ounces) large croutons
Grated Parmesan cheese to taste

*I*n a saucepan, brown the onions in the butter. Add the beef broth and simmer over low heat for 15 minutes. Pour into individual serving bowls. Top each portion with croutons and Parmesan cheese and serve.

Makes 4 servings

Gazpacho

DEBORAH HUSS, MAKEUP ARTIST

1 green bell pepper, seeded
1 cucumber, peeled
2 stalks celery
½ yellow onion, peeled
1 tomato, peeled
1 can (16 ounces) tomato juice
1 cup chicken broth
¼ cup vegetable oil (optional)
2 tablespoons red wine vinegar
¼ teaspoon garlic powder
2 tablespoons Worcestershire sauce
1 tablespoon sugar
Black pepper to taste

*C*hop all the vegetables in a food processor or blender and combine them with all the other ingredients. Chill before serving. This will stay fresh in the refrigerator for several days.

Makes 8 servings

Iced Melon Soup with Champagne and Ginger

SHIRLEY KNIGHT, ACTRESS

5 cups coarsely chopped very ripe fresh cantaloupe or honeydew melon (about 2½ pounds)
1 tablespoon grated peeled fresh ginger
1 tablespoon fresh lemon juice
3 cups dry Champagne or sparkling wine, well chilled
2 tablespoons confectioners' sugar, or to taste
Fresh mint sprigs to garnish

Purée the melon and ginger in a food processor or blender. If you use a food processor, force the purée through a strainer set inside a bowl, pressing the solids with a wooden spoon. Stir the lemon juice into the melon purée. Cover tightly and refrigerate until well chilled, at least 2 and up to 12 hours. Chill the serving bowls at the same time. Just before serving, stir the Champagne or sparkling wine into the melon purée. Then stir in just enough of the sugar to emphasize the melon's flavor without making the soup overly sweet. Ladle into the chilled bowls and garnish with mint sprigs.

Makes 4 servings

FOUR

Salads and Dressings

"I'm so grateful to Angela and her husband Peter Shaw for periodically casting me in Murder, She Wrote *and thereby enabling me to keep my Actor's Guild health benefits. As an actress with multiple sclerosis it is difficult to find work on screen. Angela and Peter gave me the opportunity to do what I love most, to act. God bless them."*

—*Madlyn Rhue, actress*

Chinese Chicken Salad

DOTIE MOREY, ASSISTANT TO PRODUCER DAVID SHAW

¼ cup sesame seeds

3 skinless, boneless chicken breasts, cooked and shredded

1 head iceberg lettuce, washed and shredded

2 scallions, chopped

1 can (10½ ounces) mandarin oranges, well drained

½ cup sugar

½ cup rice vinegar

¼ cup vegetable oil

¼ cup sesame oil

10 wontons, cut into ¼-inch strips and fried

*T*oast the sesame seeds in a skillet for several minutes until golden brown and set aside. Place the cooked shredded chicken in the bottom of a salad bowl. Mix together the lettuce and scallions and layer over the chicken. Scatter the mandarin oranges on top of the salad, then sprinkle the toasted sesame seeds over the oranges. Combine the sugar, vinegar, vegetable oil, and sesame oil in a jar, tightly covered, and shake until all ingredients are well blended. Pour the dressing over the salad to taste. Mix well. Add the wonton strips and mix lightly. Serve immediately. The salad can be made in advance by preparing all the ingredients and storing them in separate containers in the refrigerator. Leave the wonton strips at room temperature.

Makes 4 servings

Curried Chicken Salad

VINCE MCEVEETY, DIRECTOR

2 pounds skinless, boneless chicken breasts

4 cups chicken stock

1 cup mayonnaise

*G*ently boil the chicken in the stock until tender. Let cool and cut into bite-size pieces. In a large salad bowl, mix together the mayonnaise, lemon pepper, curry powder, and

1½ teaspoons lemon pepper
1½ teaspoons curry powder
1¼ teaspoons sweet pickle juice
1 Gala apple, cored and chopped
1 Granny Smith apple, cored and
  chopped
1 cup golden raisins

pickle juice. Toss in the chicken, and chill for at least 2 hours or overnight. Just before serving, toss in the apples and raisins. Serve on a ring of cantaloupe or a bed of lettuce. Garnish with fruits in season.

Makes 8 to 10 servings

Baked Seafood Salad

TIPPI HEDREN, ACTRESS

1 cup chopped green bell pepper
½ cup chopped yellow onion
2 cups chopped celery
2 cups mayonnaise
2 cans (8 ounces each) crabmeat
2 cans (8 ounces each) shrimp,
  drained
1 can (8 ounces) lobster meat,
  drained
1 can (6 ounces) chunk or solid-
  pack tuna
1 teaspoon Worcestershire sauce
1 teaspoon salt
Black pepper to taste
Tabasco sauce to taste
½ cup potato chips

*M*ix together gently all ingredients except chips. Chill for ½ hour. Preheat the oven to 350°F. Crush the potato chips and sprinkle over the salad. Bake for ½ hour. This dish can be made a day ahead as marinating improves flavor. Serve hot or cold.

Makes 6 servings

Insalada Fritta de Mares

WAYNE ROGERS, ACTOR

2 cups fresh calamari, cleaned
2 cups bay shrimp, cooked and
  deveined
2 cups sliced fresh scungilli
1 cup olive oil
3 cloves garlic, minced
Juice of 2 lemons
2 shallots, sliced
Salt and black pepper to taste
2 cans (8 ounces each) artichoke
  hearts, drained and quartered
1 cup sliced mushrooms
1 jar (8 ounces) pimientos,
  drained
4 stalks celery, finely chopped
1 can (5¾ ounces) black olives,
  drained and sliced
2 tablespoons capers
3 lemon wedges
Chopped fresh parsley to garnish

In a 4-quart pot, boil the calamari for 45 seconds. Remove from the pan and slice into strips. Place the calamari, shrimp, and raw scungilli in a high-sided dish. Add the olive oil, garlic, lemon juice, shallots, salt, and pepper. Marinate overnight in the refrigerator. Two hours before serving, add the artichoke hearts, mushrooms, pimientos, celery, olives, and capers. Stir. Drain off the excess olive oil. Serve on a bed of lettuce on a large platter. Squeeze fresh lemon wedges over the salad and garnish with parsley. Keep chilled until ready to serve.

Makes 6 servings

Broccoli Salad

CYNNIE TROUP, SCRIPT SUPERVISOR

1 cup sesame seeds
2 green apples, cored and chopped
  but not peeled
1 head broccoli, stalks discarded
  and florets finely chopped
1 white onion, finely chopped
1 cup mayonnaise
2 tablespoons lemon juice

*T*oast the sesame seeds in a skillet for several minutes until golden brown. In a large bowl, toss together the apples, broccoli, onion, and sesame seeds. In a small bowl, mix the mayonnaise with the lemon juice, drizzle over the salad, and toss to coat.

Makes 4 servings

Cabbage Salad

NANCY HOPEWELL, STAND-IN

½ head cabbage, shredded
1 can (4 ounces) green peas
1 can (4 ounces) shrimp
½ cup diced celery
3 scallions, finely chopped
2 large eggs, hard-boiled and
  chopped
Juice of 1 lemon
Salt and black pepper to taste
½ cup mayonnaise

*T*oss together the cabbage, peas, shrimp, celery, scallions, and eggs. Season with lemon juice, salt, and pepper, and gently stir in the mayonnaise.

Makes 4 servings

Caesar Salad

JESSICA WALTER, ACTRESS

3 cloves garlic, minced
6 tablespoons olive oil
2 tablespoons white wine vinegar
1 tablespoon Dijon mustard
1½ teaspoons Worcestershire sauce
¾ teaspoon salt
¾ teaspoon black pepper
1½ teaspoons lemon juice
2 large eggs, coddled
1 head romaine lettuce, washed
  and torn
½ cup croutons
4 anchovy fillets, chopped
¼ cup grated Parmesan cheese

*I*n a small bowl, soak the garlic in the olive oil for 3 hours. Then whisk in the vinegar, mustard, Worcestershire sauce, salt, pepper, lemon juice, and eggs. Toss in the lettuce. Sprinkle the croutons, anchovy fillets, and Parmesan cheese over the top and serve.

Makes 4 servings

Spicy Caesar Salad

DEDEE PFEIFFER, ACTRESS

4 slices sourdough bread, cut into
  1-inch squares
¼ cup olive oil
Juice of 1 lemon
5 cloves garlic, minced
1 heaping teaspoon dry mustard
¼ teaspoon Worcestershire sauce

*P*reheat the broiler or the oven to 450°F. Broil the bread or bake on a cookie sheet until golden brown. Set aside. In a large salad bowl, mix the oil and lemon juice. The mixture should be a little tart, but not too oily. Add the garlic and mustard. Stir in the Worcestershire sauce until the mixture turns a

1 head romaine lettuce, washed
  and torn
¾ cup grated Parmesan cheese
Black pepper to taste

medium brown color. Toss in the lettuce,
Parmesan cheese, croutons, and pepper. Mix
well and enjoy.

Makes 4 servings

Cucumber Salad

CAROL LUPO, WARDROBE

¼ cup cider vinegar
1 tablespoon honey
1 tablespoon chopped fresh dill
Cayenne pepper to taste
Ground cloves to taste
Smoked yeast to taste (available
  in health food stores)
4 cucumbers, scrubbed and thinly
  sliced

Combine all the ingredients except the
cucumbers in a large jar. Cover and shake
well. Drop the sliced cucumbers into the jar.
Do not crowd. Cover the jar tightly. Turn gently upside down and back several times to coat
the cucumbers evenly. Chill for 24 hours,
turning jar upside down from time to time.
Serve cold.

Makes 4 servings

Russian Cucumber Salad

GLORIA MONTEMAYOR, HAIRSTYLIST

4 medium cucumbers, peeled and
  sliced
1 pint sour cream
1 tablespoon dried dill
Salt and black pepper to taste

Combine the cucumbers and sour cream in
a large bowl. Sprinkle in the dill and season with salt and pepper. Make at least 2
hours ahead of time to allow the flavors to
blend. This dish can be made the night before
and chilled.

Makes 4 servings

Warm Francesca Salad

BEN MASTERS, ACTOR

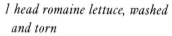

1 head romaine lettuce, washed and torn

2 small heads radicchio, washed and torn

2 small heads Belgian endive, washed and torn

6 ounces goat cheese, crumbled

½ pound bacon, cooked and crumbled, drippings reserved

2 cloves garlic, sliced into slivers

2 large leeks (white parts only), halved lengthwise and julienned

¼ cup fresh lemon juice

½ cup balsamic vinegar

Toss the lettuce, radicchio, and endive together in a serving bowl. Layer the cheese and bacon over the lettuce. In a saucepan, sauté the garlic and leeks in the reserved bacon drippings until soft. Add the lemon juice and vinegar to the saucepan and heat until just warm. Pour over the salad and serve.

Makes 6 servings

Sesame Seed Green Salad

ROBIN BEAUCHESNE, MAKEUP ARTIST

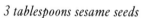

3 tablespoons sesame seeds

2 heads romaine lettuce, washed and chopped

1 pound spinach leaves, chopped

3 tomatoes, seeded and cut into wedges

½ cup small sweet onion rings

1 teaspoon salt

¼ teaspoon black pepper

Toast the sesame seeds in a skillet for several minutes until the seeds turn golden brown. Set aside. Combine the lettuce, spinach, tomato wedges, onion rings, and sesame seeds. Toss well and place in the refrigerator. Combine the salt, pepper, and dry mustard in a small mixing bowl. Stir in the vinegar and honey. Add the oil gradually, beating with a rotary beater. Chill well. Combine

½ teaspoon dry mustard
3 tablespoons vinegar, any type
1 tablespoon honey
⅓ cup vegetable oil
2 cups herb-seasoned croutons

the salad dressing and croutons with the salad and toss well. Serve immediately.

Makes 8 servings

Greek Salad

WINGS HAUSER, ACTOR

2 cloves garlic, minced
12 mushrooms, diced
1 tablespoon butter
1 pound feta cheese, crumbled
3 red onions, chopped
2 tablespoons olive oil
6 tomatoes, sliced into ¼-inch
  sections
4 avocados, peeled, seeded, and
  chopped
½ cup chopped fresh parsley

Fry the garlic and mushrooms in the butter and set aside. Mix together the cheese, onions, olive oil, tomatoes, avocados, and parsley. Place the mixture on individual serving plates and pour the fried garlic and mushroom mixture over the tops.

Makes 6 servings

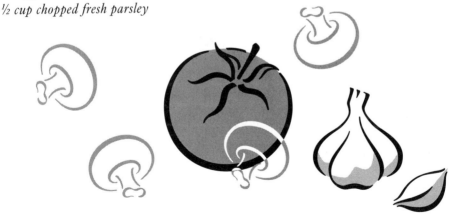

Fresh Tomato Provençal Salad and Dressing

JEAN-LOUIS DELEZENNE, CATERING CHEF

3 medium fresh tomatoes
2 shallots, finely chopped
¼ cup chopped fresh parsley
1 small sweet onion, chopped
3 ounces herbed goat cheese, crumbled
⅔ cup olive oil
⅓ cup red wine vinegar
1 tablespoon Dijon mustard
1 teaspoon mayonnaise
Tabasco sauce to taste
Salt and black pepper to taste

Mix together the tomatoes, shallots, parsley, onion, and cheese in a large serving bowl. Mix together the remaining ingredients in a separate small bowl and then toss together with the salad. Prepare at least 2 hours before serving. This can be refrigerated. Serve with French bread.

Makes 2 servings

Layered Spinach and Egg Salad

HEIDI KLING, ACTRESS

¾ pound spinach, washed, drained, and chopped
Salt and black pepper to taste
12 large eggs, hard-boiled and chopped
8 slices bacon, cooked and crumbled
1 head romaine or iceberg lettuce, washed and chopped

In a large bowl that can be securely sealed, layer the spinach, salt and pepper, eggs, and crumbled bacon. Layer the lettuce and

8 scallions, sliced
1 package (10 ounces) frozen peas
1 cup mayonnaise
1 cup ranch dressing
1½ cups shredded Cheddar cheese

season with additional salt and pepper if desired. Layer the scallions and peas. Mix together the mayonnaise and dressing and pour over the salad. Top with the cheese. Seal the bowl tightly and chill overnight before serving.

Makes 8 servings

Salad Salsa

JOSEE NORMAND, HAIRSTYLIST

1 head iceberg lettuce, washed and
  chopped
¼ pound mushrooms, sliced (about
  1 cup)
1 can (16 ounces) three-bean
  salad (green, yellow, and kidney), drained
1 can (7 ounces) black olives,
  drained and chopped
1 scallion, chopped with ends
  removed
½ cup chopped cilantro or to taste
1 pint cherry tomatoes, chopped
1 cup shredded Cheddar cheese
  (optional)
2 cups crumbled tortilla chips
1 cup salsa, homemade or in a jar
1 cup ranch dressing

𝒥n a large salad bowl, combine the lettuce, mushrooms, beans, olives, scallions, cilantro, and tomatoes. Add cheese, if using, and crumbled tortilla chips. Toss gently. In a separate bowl, mix together the salsa and ranch dressing and pour over the salad.

Makes 8 servings

Cold Cranberry Salad

MERCEDES JANE, STAND-IN

4 cups washed cranberries
2 red apples, cored and chopped
  but not peeled
2 oranges, peeled and chopped
1 cup chopped walnuts
2 cups sugar
1 package (6 ounces) lemon
  Jell-O mix

In a large bowl, mix together the cranberries, apples, oranges, and walnuts. Add the sugar and mix until the sugar is dissolved. In a separate bowl, dissolve the Jell-O mix in 2 cups warm water. Add 1 cup cold water. Mix well and refrigerate, but do not let it set. Combine the Jell-O and mixed fruit in a 1½-quart mold and let it set in the refrigerator for at least 4 hours.

Makes 8 servings

Orange Salad

GLORIA MONTEMAYOR, HAIRSTYLIST

12 Valencia oranges, peeled, seed-
  ed, and cut into ¼-inch slices
8 cloves garlic, minced
2 tablespoons olive oil

Place the oranges and garlic in an 8-inch soufflé dish. Cover with the olive oil. Chill for up to 3 hours, stirring every hour. Serve at room temperature. This can be made 1 day in advance if necessary.

Makes 10 servings

Strawberry Salad

BRAD WHITE, CRAFT SERVICES

1¼ cups water
2 packages (6 ounces each)
  strawberry Jell-O mix
2 bananas, mashed
1 can (8 ounces) crushed pineapple
2 packages (16 ounces each)
  frozen sweetened strawberries,
  thawed
1 pint sour cream, stirred in
  container

*B*oil the water and add the Jell-O mix. Stir until dissolved. Add the mashed bananas, pineapple, and strawberries with their juices and blend. Pour half the mixture into a serving dish or a gelatin mold and chill until firm. Cover and set aside the remaining half of the mixture: do not chill. Spread the sour cream over the chilled half, then pour the rest of the Jell-O mixture over the sour cream. Chill again, for 1½ hours. Serve cold.

Makes 8 servings

Sweet Potato Salad

KIM AND SHERRY KIRCHBAUM, SET PAINTERS

3½ pounds canned sweet potatoes,
  drained and chopped
1 jar (18 ounces) barbecue sauce
1½ cups mayonnaise
8 scallions, chopped
8 stalks celery, chopped
8 large eggs, hard boiled and sliced

*M*ix together all the ingredients, reserving 2 eggs. Garnish the top of the salad with these.

Makes 8 servings

Reception Salad

LEN EARLY, CARPENTER

1 can (8 ounces) crushed
pineapple, drained, juice
reserved
1 package (6 ounces) lemon
Jell-O mix
1 cup whipping cream
1 cup chopped walnuts
3 stalks celery, chopped
8 ounces cream cheese, softened

*B*oil the pineapple juice, add the Jell-O mix, and stir until dissolved. Chill in the freezer for 15 minutes, or until slightly firm. Whip the whipping cream in a large bowl and add the pineapple, nuts, celery, and cream cheese. Mix well. Add the Jell-O. Pour into a glass baking dish and chill until firm.

Makes 8 servings

Chilled Asparagus and Vinaigrette

LEANN HUNLEY, ACTRESS

1 pound fresh asparagus, ends
trimmed
¼ cup fresh lemon juice
¾ cup olive oil
2 tablespoons Dijon mustard
2 medium tomatoes, cored and
diced
⅓ cup chopped fresh basil
2 tablespoons chopped capers

*I*n a large pot, steam the asparagus for 5 minutes, until tender. Remove from the heat, drain, and chill. Whip the lemon juice, olive oil, and mustard with a whisk until thoroughly mixed. Add the tomatoes, basil, and capers and chill. Pour half the dressing over the asparagus and serve. Leftover dressing can be used on salads or any fresh steamed vegetable.

Makes 4 servings

French Dressing

FRANK MCNAIR, SECURITY GUARD

1 can (10¾ ounces) tomato soup,
  undiluted
¾ cup red wine vinegar
½ cup canola oil
¼ cup sugar
1 tablespoon Worcestershire sauce
1½ teaspoons dry onion or onion
  salt
1 teaspoon salt
1 tablespoon mustard
1 teaspoon paprika

*C*ombine all the ingredients and mix well. Store in the refrigerator and use on any salad.

Makes 2 cups

Low-Cholesterol Creamy Dressing

PAULINE BRAILSFORD, ACTRESS

½ cup nonfat cottage cheese
½ cup nonfat plain yogurt
1 tablespoon white wine vinegar
1 tablespoon Dijon mustard
¼ teaspoon NutraSweet
Salt and black pepper to taste

*P*rocess all the ingredients in a blender or food processor until smooth. For a variation, substitute anchovy paste for the mustard. For a fruit salad, omit the vinegar, mustard, and seasoning, substituting 1 tablespoon lemon juice and a handful of fresh mint leaves.

Makes 1 cup

Poppy Seed Salad Dressing

BRYAN RODGERS, PROP MASTER

1½ cups sugar
2 teaspoons salt
2 teaspoons dry mustard
⅔ cup white vinegar
3 tablespoons onion juice
2 cups mild-tasting oil
3 tablespoons poppy seeds

*M*ix together the sugar, salt, mustard, and vinegar. Add the onion juice. Add the oil slowly, beating constantly until thick. Add the poppy seeds and beat for a few minutes longer. Store in a cool place.

Makes 2 cups

Tahini Dressing

SUSAN BLAKELY, ACTRESS

1 cup tahini
⅓ cup water
Juice of 3 lemons
4 cloves garlic
2 tablespoons soy sauce
2 tablespoons honey

*P*lace all the ingredients in a food processor and blend until smooth. This will keep in the refrigerator for up to 2 weeks. The dressing will thicken as it sits, but can be thinned with water, if desired.

Makes 1½ cups

Main Courses

"I always loved doing Murder, She Wrote. *I usually played the 'bad' girl. One time, I asked Angela if I couldn't play the heroine for once. She slyly reminded me that the 'bad' girl gets all the good lines and great clothes. We had a good laugh about that and I was always delighted to be invited back as a guest star. What a joy that show was!"*
— *Susan Blakely, actress*

Beef Bourguignon

RON VARGAS, DIRECTOR OF PHOTOGRAPHY

1½ pounds boneless beef, cut into
  1-inch cubes
2 slices bacon, cooked, drippings
  reserved
1 can (10¾ ounces) beef broth
1 cup burgundy wine
1 clove garlic, minced
1 bay leaf
2 tablespoons chopped parsley
12 pearl onions, peeled

*J*n a deep pan or Dutch oven brown the beef in the bacon drippings. Crumble the reserved bacon and add to the pan. Add the broth, wine, garlic, bay leaf, and parsley. Cover and cook over low heat for 1 hour, stirring occasionally. Add the onions and cook for 1 additional hour or until tender. Remove bay leaf before serving. Serve with rice, potatoes, or noodles.

Makes 4 servings

Beef Shish Kebob

BARBARA MCHUGH, WARDROBE

16 cherry tomatoes
2 yellow onions, coarsely chopped
1 green bell pepper, coarsely
  chopped
1 red bell pepper, coarsely chopped
16 mushrooms, whole
2 pounds beef, cut into 2-inch
  cubes
2 stalks celery, coarsely chopped
1 cup prepared French dressing

*O*n skewers, alternate tomatoes, onions, peppers, mushrooms, beef, and celery. Place the skewers in a long pan and cover with French dressing. Broil for 20 minutes, turning once. Serve with rice. Pour a mixture of French dressing and pan juices over the rice. This goes well with crusty French bread and salad.

Makes 8 servings

Beef Stew

BUFFY SNYDER, KEY COSTUMER

1½ pounds beef pot roast,
  with bone
3 yellow onions, chopped
2 cups chopped celery
Salt and black pepper to taste
Bouquet garni with thyme, marjoram, rosemary, oregano, and bay
  leaf to taste
1 can (28 ounces) whole tomatoes,
  finely chopped
1 can (8 ounces) tomato sauce
3 tablespoons chopped parsley
3 carrots, chopped
1 can (8 ounces) whole kernel
  corn (optional)
¼ cup picante sauce (optional)
½ cup lentils, cooked (optional)

In a Dutch oven or large pot, brown the pot roast, onions, and celery. Cover the roast with water and add the salt, pepper, bouquet garni, tomatoes, tomato sauce, and parsley. Cook over low heat for 3 hours. Remove the meat, debone, and cut into small pieces. Return the meat to the pot and add the carrots. Add the corn, picante, and lentils, if using. Continue cooking for another ½ hour.

Makes 6 servings

Beef Teriyaki

RICHARD A. CATABONA, SECURITY

¼ cup soy sauce
⅓ cup honey
2 tablespoons sugar
1 clove garlic, minced
½ teaspoon finely minced fresh peeled ginger
1½ pounds beef tenderloin or lean pork, sliced thin

In a large bowl, combine the soy sauce, honey, sugar, garlic, and ginger. Mix well. Add the beef or pork and let marinate overnight in the refrigerator. Preheat the oven to 350°F. In a large roasting pan place the meat in a single layer and bake for 20 minutes, or until the meat is done. Baste with the leftover marinade occasionally. This dish is also excellent grilled over charcoal.

Makes 4 servings

Boeuf à la Chicarrone

RICHARD YÑIGUEZ, ACTOR

2 Spanish onions, chopped
1 can (4½ ounces) enchilada sauce, any kind
Mexican or Spanish seasoning to taste
2 pounds fatless pork rinds
1 pound ground filet mignon

Boil onions in 2½ cups water until the onions are melting into a broth, about 20 minutes. Add the enchilada sauce and Mexican seasoning. Stir in the pork rinds and simmer for 5 to 10 minutes. The rinds will soak up the onion broth and swell, absorbing the flavor and enhancing the dish. Form the beef into patties and fry or grill them. Serve the pork rinds spooned over the filets and with steamed vegetables on the side.

Makes 2 servings

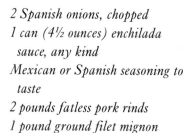

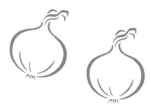

Hungarian Goulash

ERIC VESPER, DOLLY GRIP

4 medium yellow onions, chopped

4 tablespoons vegetable oil

2 tablespoons flour

1½ pounds lean stewing beef, cut into 1-inch pieces

1½ pounds lean pork roast, cut into 1-inch pieces

2 tablespoons paprika

2 cloves garlic, minced

2 teaspoons salt

1 cup tomato purée

2 cups beef broth

¼ teaspoon black pepper

½ teaspoon dried thyme

1 bay leaf

½ teaspoon parsley flakes

Over medium-high heat, brown the onions in the oil. Sprinkle the flour over the cubed meat, add to the onions, and cook until evenly browned. Lower heat and add the rest of the ingredients. Simmer until the meat is very tender, at least 1½ hours. Serve over rice or noodles.

Makes 6 servings

Italian Delight Goulash

BEVERLY SEIFERT, DRIVER TO MS. LANSBURY

2 pounds ground beef
Salt and black pepper to taste
1 large yellow onion, chopped
1 green bell pepper, chopped
1 clove garlic, minced
9⅓ cups tomato sauce
1 can (10¾ ounces) tomato soup,
 undiluted
1 can (16 ounces) whole kernel
 corn
1 can (16 ounces) creamed corn
1 can (4 ounces) sliced mushrooms
 and juice
1 can (7 ounces) pimientos,
 chopped
1 teaspoon sugar
1 teaspoon chili powder
¾ pound egg noodles
2 cups shredded cheese, any type

In a large skillet, brown the meat and season with salt and pepper to taste. Pour off the grease. Add the onion, green pepper, and garlic. Add the tomato sauce, tomato soup, whole corn, creamed corn, mushrooms and juice, pimientos, sugar, and chili powder. Bring to a boil, reduce heat, and simmer for 15 to 20 minutes. Meanwhile, boil a pot of water and cook the noodles until just tender. Drain. Preheat the oven to 350°F. Place the noodles in a large, ovenproof casserole dish and cover with the goulash. Sprinkle cheese evenly over the top and bake for ½ hour or until heated through.

Makes 8 servings

Spinach Meat Loaf

KATE MULGREW, ACTRESS

2 packages (10 ounces each)
  frozen spinach
2 yellow onions, diced
1 package (2 ounces) Pepperidge
  Farm stuffing
2 tablespoons butter, melted
1 green bell pepper, diced
1 red bell pepper, diced
5 stalks celery, diced
2 tablespoons diced fresh parsley
1½ pounds ground beef
1 tomato, cored and diced
1 large egg
½ teaspoon Tabasco sauce
1 tablespoon Worcestershire sauce
Salt and black pepper to taste
¼ pound mozzarella cheese,
  shredded
1 tablespoon steak sauce (optional)

Preheat the oven to 350°F. Prepare the frozen spinach according to package directions and drain. Set aside. Sauté the onions with the stuffing in the melted butter for 2 minutes. Add the bell peppers, celery, and parsley. Sauté for an additional 2 minutes. Remove from heat and mix with the cooked spinach. Set aside. In a large mixing bowl, mix the ground beef, tomato, egg, Tabasco sauce, and Worcestershire sauce. Season with salt and pepper to taste. Flatten the ground beef mixture out on a flat surface. Spread the spinach mixture over it and sprinkle the cheese on top. Roll this up into a meat loaf and place in a buttered casserole dish. Indent the meat loaf on top and pour on the steak sauce if desired. Bake for 1 hour. Serve with mashed potatoes and steamed green beans.

Makes 4 servings

Milanese con Papas

LEON SINGER, ACTOR

2 pounds top-quality round steak,
  sliced ⅛-inch thick
1 cup plain dry breadcrumbs
½ teaspoon salt
¼ teaspoon black pepper
¼ teaspoon garlic powder
1 bay leaf (optional)
2 large eggs, lightly beaten
2½ tablespoons vegetable oil
¼ cup guacamole (optional)

Pound the meat over a hard surface with a flat instrument. Do not use a regular kitchen meat pounder; it can make holes in the thin slices of meat. A flat piece of wood, the bottom of a heavy pot, or even a rolling pin will work. Cut into serving-size pieces and set aside. Place the breadcrumbs, salt, pepper, garlic powder, and bay leaf in a blender or food processor and pulverize. Dip pieces of steak into the beaten egg, then pat crumb mixture onto each, pressing firmly. Heat a large skillet, add vegetable oil to coat the bottom, and rapidly fry the steak pieces on both sides. Do not overcook or allow coating or steaks to burn. Serve with potatoes and garnish with guacamole, if desired.

Makes 4 servings

Old-Fashioned Scrapple

LUCINDA WEIST, ACTRESS

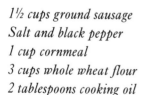

1½ cups ground sausage
Salt and black pepper
1 cup cornmeal
3 cups whole wheat flour
2 tablespoons cooking oil

In a heavy pan, boil the sausage in 3 quarts water until done. Remove the meat with a slotted spoon and set aside. Return the broth to a boil and season with salt and pepper to taste. Add the cornmeal and flour to the broth,

stirring constantly until it begins to thicken. Then add the meat and continue stirring. The mixture should have the consistency of cream of wheat. Cook slowly over medium heat for ½ hour. Pour into a casserole dish to cool and allow to set. When cold, slice in ¼-inch-thick pieces and fry in oil until brown and crusty on both sides. Serve hot with molasses syrup.

Makes 6 to 8 servings

Oklahoma-Style Tortillas

BEN GRAHAM, LIGHTING TECHNICIAN

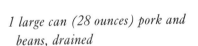

1 large can (28 ounces) pork and beans, drained
2 cans (8 ounces each) tomato sauce
6 hot dogs, sliced ¼-inch thick
2 large yellow onions, chopped
2 green bell peppers, seeded and diced
8 to 10 scallions, chopped
1 hot or mild pepper, chopped (optional)
½ cup chopped cilantro
8 large flour tortillas

In a 4-quart pot, mix together all ingredients except the tortillas. Cook over low heat for 1½ to 2 hours, stirring periodically. Heat the large tortillas in a skillet and place on individual plates. Ladle the filling onto half of each tortilla and fold over.

Makes 8 servings

Cuban Picadillo

MARIA CANALS, ACTRESS

1 medium yellow onion, chopped

1 medium green bell pepper, chopped

1 tablespoon olive oil

2 cloves garlic, minced

1 can (6 ounces) tomato sauce

⅓ cup water

1 teaspoon ground cumin

1 teaspoon dried oregano

2 bay leaves

1 pound lean ground beef

½ cup dry red or white wine

1 envelope (1½ ounces) Spanish seasonings

½ cup pitted olives stuffed with pimiento (optional)

¼ cup raisins

1 large potato, cubed

½ cup vegetable oil

Sauté the onion and green pepper in the olive oil. Add the garlic and cook over medium-low heat until softened. Add the tomato sauce, water, cumin, oregano, and bay leaves. Add the meat and stir well. Add the wine, Spanish seasonings, olives, and raisins. Mix well. Cover and simmer for ½ hour, stirring occasionally, until the liquids are condensed. Fluff with a fork and set aside. In a separate skillet, fry the diced potato in the vegetable oil over medium heat. Make sure the oil is very hot before adding potatoes—these will serve as a garnish over the picadillo. When potatoes are done, drain on a paper towel and scatter over the picadillo. Serve with white rice.

Makes 6 servings

Pot Roast and Vegetables

ANNE MEARA, ACTRESS

3 to 4 pounds bottom pot roast
1½ cups flour
⅓ cup vegetable oil
3 cloves garlic, minced
4 medium yellow onions, chopped
2 bay leaves
1 pound carrots, roughly chopped
6 potatoes, cubed
6 stalks celery, roughly chopped
1 yellow bell pepper, chopped
1 red bell pepper, chopped
1 green bell pepper, chopped
1 envelope (2 ounces) instant
* brown gravy mix*

Preheat the oven to 350°F. Coat the meat with flour. In a deep pan or Dutch oven, sear the meat in the vegetable oil on all sides. Add the garlic, 1 chopped onion, and bay leaves. Cover the meat with boiling water. Cover the pot and place in the oven to cook for 2 hours. In a separate pot, boil the remaining onions, carrots, potatoes, celery, and peppers for ½ hour. Drain the vegetables and add them to the meat after it has been cooking for 2 hours. Cover and cook for another 3 hours. Boil 1 cup water and dissolve the instant gravy mix in it. Add this mixture to the meat and vegetables and cook for 1 hour more. Total cooking time is 5 hours.

Makes 8 servings

Sautéed Steakburger with Mushroom Sauce

CAROL LUPO, WARDROBE

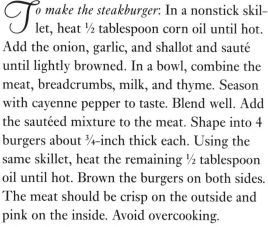

STEAKBURGER

1 tablespoon corn oil

1 small yellow onion, minced

2 large cloves garlic, minced

1 shallot, minced

1 pound ground top sirloin

¼ cup fine dry breadcrumbs

⅛ cup low-fat milk

¼ teaspoon dried thyme

Cayenne pepper to taste

MUSHROOM SAUCE

1½ tablespoons corn oil

1 shallot, minced

1 clove garlic, minced

½ pound fresh mushrooms,
  trimmed and sliced

1½ tablespoons unbleached flour

1 cup beef stock, heated

2 tablespoons dry vermouth or
  white wine (optional)

¼ teaspoon dried thyme

Cayenne pepper

½ teaspoon curry powder

Freshly chopped parsley to garnish

To make the steakburger: In a nonstick skillet, heat ½ tablespoon corn oil until hot. Add the onion, garlic, and shallot and sauté until lightly browned. In a bowl, combine the meat, breadcrumbs, milk, and thyme. Season with cayenne pepper to taste. Blend well. Add the sautéed mixture to the meat. Shape into 4 burgers about ¾-inch thick each. Using the same skillet, heat the remaining ½ tablespoon oil until hot. Brown the burgers on both sides. The meat should be crisp on the outside and pink on the inside. Avoid overcooking.

To make the sauce: Begin preparing the sauce about 10 minutes before the burgers are ready. In a large nonstick skillet, heat the oil until hot. Add the shallot and garlic and sauté 1 minute. Add the mushrooms. Sauté for 3 minutes until lightly browned. Sprinkle the flour over the mixture and cook for 2 more minutes, stirring well so that the flour cooks through. Combine the stock and vermouth or wine and add to the skillet, stirring constantly. Add the thyme, cayenne pepper to taste, and curry powder. Simmer, uncovered, for 2 minutes. Pour the sauce over the steakburgers. Garnish with the parsley and serve.

Makes 4 servings

Spicy Garlic Steak Tacos

RICH SICKLER, SECOND ASSISTANT DIRECTOR

5 cloves garlic, minced
Spike seasoning
2 marbled ribeye steaks
Salt and black pepper to taste
2 medium avocados, peeled,
  seeded, and mashed
3 tablespoons salsa
12 flour tortillas
1 large tomato, cored and diced
½ head red leaf lettuce, torn
¼ red onion, chopped
2 ounces Monterey Jack cheese,
  shredded
Taco sauce to taste

Mix together the garlic and Spike seasoning to taste. Spread this mixture on the steaks. Season with salt and pepper and cover. Refrigerate while you prepare the grill with mesquite charcoal. When the coals are white-hot, put the steaks on. Grill on both sides, turning often, for 8 minutes, or until medium rare. Remove and slice into thin strips.

In a bowl, combine the mashed avocados and salsa. Heat the tortillas on the grill, flipping frequently. Remove the tortillas and fill with steak strips, avocados, tomatoes, lettuce, onion, and cheese and top with taco sauce. Fold one end over (to seal juices in) and roll up.

Makes 12 tacos

Easy Braised Pork

PENNY FULLER, ACTRESS

1 pork roast, about 4 pounds
6 tablespoons olive oil
Salt and black pepper to taste
2 tablespoons water
5 cloves garlic
30 fresh sage leaves
2 sprigs fresh mint

In a Dutch oven, brown the roast well in 4 tablespoons of the olive oil. Season with salt and pepper. Discard the used oil and add the remaining 2 tablespoons olive oil, water, garlic, sage, and mint. Cover and cook over low heat for 3 hours. Add water, if needed. Baste occasionally.

Makes 6 servings

Taco Pie

KATHERINE WALLACE, EXECUTIVE ASSISTANT TO MS. LANSBURY

½ cup cornmeal
1 teaspoon salt
3 tablespoons sugar
1 pound beef, cubed or ground
½ green bell pepper, chopped
½ red bell pepper, chopped
1 medium-sized yellow onion,
  chopped
¾ cup chopped cilantro
½ package (1 ounce) taco
  seasoning mix
⅔ cup mayonnaise
1 cup sour cream
1 tablespoon parsley flakes
1 large tomato, cored and sliced
1½ cups shredded Cheddar cheese

In a saucepan, boil 1 cup water. Add the cornmeal, ½ cup cold water, salt, and sugar. Cook for 10 minutes until the cornmeal is firm. Let the mixture cool slightly, then press into a 9-inch pie plate. In a skillet, brown the beef, then drain off the fat, add the bell peppers and onion to the pan and sauté until tender. Then add ½ cup cilantro and the taco seasoning mix and stir well. Place the filling mixture in the cornmeal pie shell. Preheat the oven to 350°F. Mix the remaining ¼ cup cilantro, the mayonnaise, sour cream, and parsley flakes. Spread on top of the filling in the pie shell. Top with sliced tomatoes and cheese. Bake for ½ hour.

Makes 6 servings

Poultry Meat Loaf

CURTIS BLANCK, ACTOR

2 pounds ground chicken or
  ground turkey
1 large egg
1 can (4 ounces) tomato sauce
½ cup plain dry breadcrumbs
½ carrot, chopped

Preheat the oven to 375°F. Mix together the ground meat, egg, tomato sauce, breadcrumbs, carrot, salt, pepper, and parsley flakes and form into a meat loaf. Place the meat loaf in a lightly greased shallow baking dish. In a small bowl, mix the ketchup and

¼ teaspoon salt (optional)
Freshly ground black pepper
  to taste
¼ teaspoon parsley flakes
⅓ cup ketchup
4 tablespoons light Karo syrup

Karo syrup together. Generously brush this mixture over the top and sides of the meat loaf, every 15 minutes throughout baking. Bake for 45 minutes to 1 hour. Serve with Butternut Squash Mashed Potatoes (see Index).

Makes 6 servings

Vegetarian Meat Loaf

THOM BIERDZ, ACTOR

2 cups tomato purée
¾ cup ketchup
3 cups ground unsalted nuts,
  any type except peanuts
3½ cups cooked white or brown
  rice
2 cups shredded cheese, any type
2 tablespoons dried sage
1 tablespoon dried thyme
2 tablespoons dried basil
1 teaspoon salt
1 teaspoon garlic powder
1 teaspoon black pepper
1 cup chopped celery
5 carrots, chopped
1 cup chopped, cooked butternut
  squash

*P*reheat the oven to 350°F. Mix together the tomato purée and ketchup. In a separate bowl, mix together the nuts, rice, ½ cup of the cheese, sage, thyme, basil, salt, garlic powder, and pepper. Stir in half of the tomato and ketchup mixture. Add the celery, carrots, and squash. Mix well and mold into a greased loaf pan. Cover with aluminum foil and bake for 50 minutes. Uncover, top with the remaining half of the tomato and ketchup mixture and the remaining 1½ cups cheese. Bake for 20 minutes more. Serve hot.

Makes 8 servings

Spicy Chuck Roast

KEVIN CORCORAN, FIRST ASSISTANT DIRECTOR

1 tablespoon vegetable oil
3 pounds chuck roast
1 cup salsa, homemade or
* from a jar*
1 tablespoon soy sauce
1 tablespoon packed light or dark
* brown sugar*
1 teaspoon salt
¼ teaspoon garlic powder
6 carrots, sliced
4 potatoes, quartered

Heat the oil in a large deep skillet. Brown the meat on both sides. In a separate pan, mix together the salsa, soy sauce, brown sugar, salt, and garlic powder. Pour this mixture over the meat. Cover and cook over medium heat for 2 hours. Add water, if necessary. Add the carrots and potatoes, cover, and cook an additional ½ hour to 45 minutes.

Makes 6 servings

Carnitas (Spicy Taco Filling)

TONY GUASTELLA, SET DRESSING LEADMAN

1¼ ounces taco seasoning mix
2 teaspoons Tabasco sauce
Salt and black pepper to taste
1 pork butt roast, 2 to 3 pounds

Fill a 5-quart Crock-Pot one-quarter full with water. Stir in the taco seasoning, Tabasco sauce, salt, and pepper. Place the roast in the Crock-Pot, adding more water to cover the meat if necessary. Cook over high heat for 7 to 8 hours. Remove the meat and place it on a cookie sheet. Preheat the oven to 400°F. Shred the meat into pieces (it will break apart easily) and season with additional Tabasco sauce if desired. Bake for 20 minutes. Use the meat to make burritos or tacos.

Makes 6 servings

Flemish Pork with Beer

RON MASAK, ACTOR

3 tablespoons butter
2½ pounds pork shoulder, diced
Salt and black pepper to taste
½ cup beer
½ cup boiling water
1 teaspoon crushed dried rosemary
1 jar (16 ounces) pearl onions
2 cups pork or chicken broth
2 packages (12 ounces each)
  frozen brussels sprouts, thawed
2 cups sliced potatoes,
  partially cooked
2 cups sliced carrots,
  partially cooked
¼ cup all-purpose flour

*I*n a large kettle, melt the butter and brown the meat. Add the salt, pepper, beer, water, and rosemary. Simmer, covered, for 45 minutes. Add the onions and simmer, covered, for another ½ hour. Add the broth, brussels sprouts, potatoes, and carrots and simmer for 25 minutes more. Blend the flour with 3 tablespoons water to make a paste and gradually stir into the pork and vegetable mixture. Stir until thickened and serve.

Makes 6 servings

Herbed Pork Tenderloin with Oven-Roasted Potatoes

JOHN MALDANADO, MAKEUP

⅓ cup olive oil
2 cloves garlic, minced
2 teaspoons crushed dried rosemary
2 teaspoons crushed dried thyme
½ teaspoon salt
¼ teaspoon black pepper
2 whole pork tenderloins, ¾ to 1
  pound each
2½ pounds new potatoes, washed
  and quartered

Preheat the oven to 375°F. In a small bowl, combine the oil, garlic, rosemary, thyme, salt, and pepper. Coat the meat with 3 tablespoons of the mixture and place in a large roasting pan. Toss the potatoes with the remaining mixture and arrange them in the pan around the roast. Cook for 35 to 40 minutes, or until a thermometer registers 155°F and the juice runs clear. Rotate the potatoes after 20 minutes. When nearly cooked, put the pan under the broiler for 5 minutes to brown. Let stand 10 minutes before slicing.

Makes 8 servings

Indiana Pork and Kraut

SUSAN VERCELLI, PRODUCTION COORDINATOR

1 tablespoon vegetable oil
1½ pounds lean, boneless pork ribs
Salt and black pepper to taste
1 Granny Smith apple, cored
  and cut into wedges
1 can (27 ounces) undrained
  sauerkraut

In a large pan, heat the vegetable oil and brown the pork. Once browned, add salt and pepper to taste. Add the apple, sauerkraut, and 1 cup water to the pot and simmer over medium heat for about 1 hour. The apple sweetens the sauerkraut. Serve with mashed potatoes.

Makes 2 servings

Spanish Pork Picadillo

WILLIAM BROCHTRUP, ACTOR

1 large onion, chopped
3½ pounds boneless pork
  tenderloin, cubed
2 cloves garlic, minced
2 tablespoons butter
2 tablespoons mild-tasting oil
1 can (16 ounces) tomato sauce
½ cup tomato-based chili sauce
1 teaspoon ground cinnamon
2 teaspoons salt
¼ teaspoon ground cumin
3 tablespoons red wine vinegar
3 tablespoons water
3 tablespoons light or dark
  brown sugar
2 scallions, chopped
1 avocado, peeled, seeded,
  and chopped
¼ cup fresh lime juice

Brown the onion, pork, and garlic in the butter and oil until the pork is cooked through. Add the tomato sauce, chili sauce, cinnamon, salt, cumin, vinegar, water, brown sugar, and scallions. Cook for 1 hour over low heat. Top with the avocado and lime juice. Serve over rice.

Makes 8 servings

Sausage and Rice Stuffing

MARTA DUBOIS, ACTRESS

½ cup white rice
1 teaspoon salt
1 yellow onion, chopped
2 cups chopped celery
4 tablespoons butter
½ teaspoon dried sweet basil
½ teaspoon salt
½ teaspoon black pepper
1 pound ground pork sausage
1 medium apple, cored and
 chopped
1½ cups milk
1 tablespoon sugar
2 large eggs

*B*oil the rice in 3 cups water, adding the salt. Reduce heat and cover. Cook for 15 minutes, drain, and set aside. Preheat the oven to 350°F. Fry the onion and celery in the butter until soft. Add the basil, salt, and pepper. In a separate pan, fry the pork sausage. Remove the fat but don't drain completely. Add the sausage to the onions and celery. Add the rice, apple, milk, sugar, and eggs. Mix well. Place in a greased baking dish and bake for ½ hour.

Makes 6 servings

Kléftiko
(Greek Herbed Lamb)

CHRISTOPHER NEAME, ACTOR

½ cup plus 2 tablespoons olive oil
½ pound yellow onions, sliced
2 pounds boned lamb from the leg
 or shoulder, cut into 1-inch cubes
½ teaspoon crushed dried rosemary
2 medium tomatoes, skinned,
 seeded, and chopped

*I*n a large flameproof casserole dish, heat 2 tablespoons olive oil and fry the onions over low heat until translucent. Add the cubed lamb and brown all sides. Add the rosemary and tomatoes and season with salt and pepper. Simmer for 15 to 25 minutes, depending on the cut—15 minutes for the shoulder, 25 min-

Salt and freshly ground black
  pepper to taste
½ pound feta cheese
2 cloves garlic, minced
½ cup chopped flat-leaf parsley
12 sheets phyllo pastry, thawed
1½ teaspoons cracked wheat or rice
1 tablespoon sesame seeds

utes for the leg. The sauce should be reduced and quite thick.

Crumble the feta with the garlic and chopped parsley and set aside. Unwrap the phyllo and place under a damp cloth, removing only 1 sheet at a time. Place 1 sheet on a work surface and brush it evenly with olive oil. Place a second sheet directly on top and brush with olive oil. Sprinkle a pinch (¼ teaspoon or less) of cracked wheat or rice over the middle of the pastry, leaving a 3-inch wide border on all sides.

Preheat the oven to 350°F. Roughly divide the meat in sixths. Spoon a portion of meat and sauce over the center of the pastry, and sprinkle with a little of the crumbled feta mixture. Fold the phyllo ends over the filling, then fold the sides inward. Roll it up, making sure the sides stay tucked in. Place the envelope, seam-side down, on an oiled or nonstick baking sheet. Brush the top with olive oil and sprinkle with sesame seeds. Continue using 2 phyllo sheets per envelope until you have used up all the filling.

Bake for ½ hour or until the 6 phyllo envelopes are golden brown. This dish was invented by and named after the Kléftiko, guerrillas of the Greek war of independence. It is said that they cooked their food over fires in pastry envelopes so that they could grab their meal and run if the need arose.

Makes 6 servings

Greek Roast Leg of Lamb

BRUCE LANSBURY, SUPERVISING PRODUCER

1 leg of lamb, 5 to 6 pounds
3 cloves garlic, sliced
Salt and black pepper to taste
Juice of 1 lemon
1 tablespoon olive oil
3 tablespoons dried oregano

Wash and dry the lamb and place it in a roasting pan. Make several incisions in the lamb with a sharp knife. Insert the slices of garlic into the incisions and season with salt and pepper. Pour the lemon juice and olive oil over the lamb. Marinate 2 to 3 hours in the refrigerator. Preheat the oven to 350°F. Sprinkle the oregano over the lamb. Bake for 2½ hours, being careful not to overcook.

Makes 8 servings

Veal or Chicken Cacciatore

MARTIN MILNER, ACTOR

2 pounds ground veal or
* ground chicken*
⅓ cup seasoned Italian
* breadcrumbs*
2 large eggs
Salt and black pepper to taste
2 tablespoons extra-virgin olive
* oil, plus extra for greasing*
4 lettuce leaves
1 yellow onion, sliced
1 green bell pepper, sliced
1 yellow bell pepper, sliced

Mix together the veal or chicken, breadcrumbs, and eggs in a bowl. Season with salt and pepper. Form into 4 patties and brown in 2 tablespoons olive oil. Place the patties on lettuce leaves in a skillet greased with olive oil to keep them from sticking. In a separate large skillet or wok, combine the onion, bell peppers, mushrooms, tomatoes, and chicken broth. Simmer until the vegetables are tender. Remove the lettuce leaves from under the meat and add the red wine to the skillet. When the vegetables are done, add them to the pan

1 red bell pepper, sliced

12 mushrooms, sliced

6 fresh Roma or plum tomatoes, cored and chopped

1 can (14½ ounces) chicken broth

¾ cup red wine

Italian parsley to garnish

with the meat and simmer together for 3 to 4 minutes. Place the patties on 4 serving plates, cover with the vegetables, and garnish with Italian parsley. Serve with crusty bread.

Makes 4 servings

Veal or Chicken Scallopini

SUZANNE WAITE, SCRIPT SUPERVISOR

1½ pounds veal cutlet or skinless chicken, trimmed, boned, pounded, and cut into 1-inch squares

1 cup flour

1 tablespoon butter

1 tablespoon oil

½ pound mushrooms, thinly sliced

2 cloves garlic, crushed

2 tablespoons chopped fresh basil

½ cup Marsala wine

2 tablespoons grated Parmesan cheese

*P*reheat the oven to 325°F. Coat the veal or chicken with the flour. Add the butter and oil to a large heated skillet. Add the veal or chicken and brown on both sides. Place the meat in a casserole dish and add the mushrooms, garlic, basil, wine, and Parmesan cheese. Mix to coat well, cover, and bake for 45 minutes.

Makes 4 servings

Capon with Wild Rice Stuffing

RAMY ZADA, ACTOR

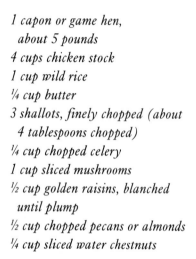

1 capon or game hen,
  about 5 pounds
4 cups chicken stock
1 cup wild rice
¼ cup butter
3 shallots, finely chopped (about
  4 tablespoons chopped)
¼ cup chopped celery
1 cup sliced mushrooms
½ cup golden raisins, blanched
  until plump
½ cup chopped pecans or almonds
¼ cup sliced water chestnuts

Clean the bird and remove the giblets. Chop the giblets and liver. Bring the chicken stock to a boil. Drop the giblets into the stock and simmer for 15 minutes. Remove the giblets from the pot and set aside. Bring the broth back to a boil, stir in the rice, and simmer until nearly tender, about ½ hour.

Preheat the oven to 450°F. Drain the rice and place in a large mixing bowl. In a skillet, melt the butter and sauté the shallots, celery, and mushrooms. Add the sautéed vegetables to the rice and mix in the giblets, raisins, pecans, and water chestnuts. Place half of this mixture in an ovenproof casserole dish. Bake for 45 minutes to 1 hour. Serve this stuffing alongside the finished bird or save it for another meal.

Use the remaining half of this mixture to stuff the bird, then truss the opening. Place the stuffed bird on a rack in a roasting pan. Roast, uncovered, at 450°F for 25 minutes per pound. Remove the stuffing and serve the stuffing separately. Allow the bird to rest 10 minutes before carving.

Makes 5 servings

Chicken Adobo

DOLORES DOMASIN, STAND-IN

1 stewing chicken, cut into pieces
½ tablespoon ground allspice
5 bay leaves
¼ yellow onion, sliced
5 cloves garlic, minced
1 tablespoon sliced peeled
 fresh ginger
¼ cup red wine vinegar
½ cup white vinegar
¼ cup soy sauce
1 chicken bouillon cube

*P*lace all the ingredients in a large saucepan. Add enough water to cover the chicken. Cover and cook over medium heat for 40 minutes, or until the chicken is tender. Serve with steamed rice.

Makes 4 servings

Chicken Breasts Grauman

WALTER GRAUMAN, DIRECTOR

6 boneless, skinless chicken breasts
1 cup low-fat, low-sodium
 Russian dressing
8 ounces chopped apricots
1 package (1½ ounces) onion
 soup mix
6 pineapple rings

*P*reheat the oven to 350°F. Arrange the chicken in a baking dish and set aside. In a bowl, mix together the Russian dressing, apricots, and onion soup mix in ¼ cup water. Pour over the chicken pieces. Cover and bake for 1 hour. Remove the cover, arrange a pineapple slice on top of each chicken breast, and bake, uncovered, for another ½ hour.

Makes 6 servings

Chicken Calvados

LEE SMITH, DIRECTOR

¼ cup salt
8 small boneless, skinless chicken
  breasts, about 2 pounds
½ cup flour
6 tablespoons butter
½ cup Calvados (apple brandy)
Juice of 1 lemon
1 tablespoon honey
4 small Granny Smith apples,
  peeled, cored, and thickly sliced

Salt the chicken, then lightly coat with flour. In a large skillet, brown the chicken slowly in the butter. Add the Calvados, lemon juice, and honey. Turn the chicken to coat on both sides. Add the apple slices. Cover and simmer for 10 to 12 minutes, until the apples are tender but still retain their shape. Remove the chicken and apples from the liquid and keep warm. Increase the heat to medium and cook the pan juices until slightly thickened, stirring often. Spoon the sauce over the chicken and serve with rice.

Makes 6 servings

Chicken Cordon Bleu

BRANDON BOYLE, PROP MAN

6 boneless, skinless chicken
  breasts, washed
2 large eggs, beaten
2 cups dry breadcrumbs
6 pieces thinly sliced ham
1 can (10¾ ounces) cream of
  mushroom soup, undiluted
Garlic salt and black pepper to
  taste
2 cups shredded mozzarella cheese

Preheat the oven to 350°F. Do not dry the chicken breasts. Dip into the eggs and then coat with breadcrumbs. Arrange the chicken in a casserole dish with a piece of ham on top of each piece. Pour the soup over the ham and chicken and season with garlic salt and black pepper. Sprinkle with cheese and bake for 1 hour.

Makes 6 servings

Chicken Cordon Gold

EILISH, DESIGNER TO MS. LANSBURY

12 boneless chicken breasts,
  pounded thin
1 cup flour
Salt and black pepper to taste
16 ounces herbed Boursin cheese
12 slices prosciutto
8 tablespoons (1 stick) butter
1 cup chicken broth
½ cup plus 2 tablespoons
  Galliano liqueur
½ pound mushrooms, sliced
¼ cup chopped fresh parsley

Coat the chicken breasts with flour mixed with salt and pepper. Layer each breast with a couple of tablespoons of herbed Boursin cheese, then one slice of prosciutto. Roll up each breast, secure it with toothpicks, and close up the ends (also with toothpicks). Brown the breasts lightly in 4 tablespoons of the butter. Pour in the broth and ½ cup of the Galliano. Cover the skillet and simmer slowly until tender, about ½ hour. In another skillet, heat the remaining 4 tablespoons butter and 2 tablespoons Galliano: add the mushrooms and sauté for 5 to 8 minutes. Add the parsley and cook for another 3 minutes: add the sauce to the chicken 5 minutes before serving. Remove the toothpicks. Serve over rice or noodles.

Makes 8 servings

Mushroom Chicken

CRAIG GADSBY, SET DECORATOR

4 skinless chicken breasts
Salt and black pepper to taste
1 pint sour cream
1 can (10¾ ounces) cream of
  mushroom soup, undiluted
¼ pound mushrooms, sliced
  (optional)
¼ pound (1 stick) butter
  or margarine
1 box (10 ounces) instant
  chicken stuffing

Preheat the oven to 350°F. Boil the chicken in a large pot, seasoned with salt and pepper. Remove when tender, about 15 minutes, and cut into cubes. Reserve the stock. In a bowl, mix together the chicken, sour cream, and mushroom soup. Arrange in a single layer in a casserole or baking dish. Sauté the mushrooms, if using, and place on top. Boil 2 cups reserved chicken stock and add the butter. Mix with the stuffing and place on top of the casserole dish. Bake, uncovered, for 1 hour.

Makes 6 servings

Chicken de Van

BARBARA MCHUGH, WARDROBE

8 or more boneless, skinless chicken
  breasts
2 tablespoons vegetable oil
4 tablespoons butter, softened
2 tablespoons flour
2½ cups milk

In a skillet, lightly brown the chicken in the vegetable oil. Set aside. In a small bowl, make a white sauce by mixing the butter, flour, milk, and sherry. Season with salt and pepper and set aside. Preheat the oven to 375°F. Butter a shallow 8 by 13-inch baking

¼ cup sherry, warmed over
  low heat
Salt and black pepper to taste
3 cups chopped broccoli, cooked
  but firm
½ cup freshly grated Romano or
  Parmesan cheese

pan. Layer the broccoli in the dish, followed by a layer of chicken. Spoon the white sauce over the chicken, and sprinkle the cheese over the sauce. Bake for 15 to 20 minutes. The cheese should get crusty on top.

Makes 4 servings

Chicken Stew, Boom Boom

FREDDIE MILLER, BOOM MAN

1 whole chicken, cut into
  serving pieces
1 small yellow onion, chopped
3 cloves garlic, minced
½ cup chopped green bell pepper
2 cups peeled, seeded, and chopped
  tomatoes
⅔ cup chicken broth
1 tablespoon paprika
1 bay leaf
2 pieces lemon peel, about
  1 inch each
½ teaspoon salt
¼ teaspoon pepper
½ teaspoon dried rosemary

*I*n a large skillet, sauté the chicken and onion. Add the garlic, bell pepper, and tomatoes. Cook over medium heat until it begins to boil. Add the chicken broth, paprika, bay leaf, lemon peel, salt, pepper, and rosemary. Cover, reduce heat to a simmer, and cook for 1 hour. Remove the chicken to another pan and keep warm. Purée the sauce with a hand mixer or in a food processor or blender. Return to the skillet, add the chicken, and heat through. Serve over bow tie noodles.

Makes 4 servings

Chicken with Rice

JAMES R. WEIS, SECOND ASSISTANT DIRECTOR

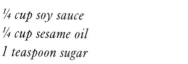

1 package (7 ounces) Minute Rice
1 can (10¾ ounces) cream of
  celery soup, undiluted
1 can (10¾ ounces) cream of
  chicken soup, undiluted
½ cup water
4 medium chicken breasts
1 package (1½ ounces) Lipton's
  Onion Soup mix

*P*reheat the oven to 325°F. Mix together the rice, cream of celery soup, cream of chicken soup, and water, and place in a 9 by 13-inch greased ovenproof dish. Place the chicken on top. Sprinkle the package of soup mix over the chicken. Cover with foil and bake for 2 hours.

Makes 4 servings

Chinese Chicken

ROD TAYLOR, ACTOR

¼ cup soy sauce
¼ cup sesame oil
1 teaspoon sugar
1 tablespoon oyster sauce
4 cloves garlic, minced
1 tablespoon grated peeled fresh
  ginger, about ½-inch
1 tablespoon cornstarch
6 to 8 chicken legs and/or thighs,
  washed
¼ cup peanut oil
1 cup chicken stock
¼ yellow onion, sliced

*I*n a medium bowl, mix together the soy sauce, sesame oil, sugar, oyster sauce, garlic, and ginger. Add the cornstarch mixed with 1 tablespoon of cold water to thicken the marinade. Place the chicken pieces in the bowl and mix to coat well. Marinate the chicken in the refrigerator for 1 to 2 hours. Remove the chicken pieces and reserve the marinade. Sauté the chicken in the peanut oil in a large skillet or wok. When browned, add the chicken stock and enough water to barely cover the chicken. Add the onion and reserved marinade and simmer for 15 minutes. When nearly

1 cup chopped broccoli
1 cup chopped mushrooms
1 green bell pepper, chopped
8 asparagus spears
2 carrots, julienned
Cilantro and scallions to garnish

ready to serve, add the broccoli, mushrooms, green pepper, asparagus, and carrots. Be sure not to overcook the vegetables. Garnish with chopped cilantro and scallions.

Makes 4 to 6 servings

Chinese Noodles with Chicken

TOM SAWYER, PRODUCER/WRITER

½ cup tahini or sesame paste (can be made by grinding up sesame seeds)
½ cup peanut butter
½ cup water
2 tablespoons chili oil
2 tablespoons sugar
¾ cup soy sauce
½ cup plus 1½ tablespoons sesame oil
2 cloves garlic, minced
¼ cup red wine vinegar
Freshly ground black pepper to taste
2 whole boneless, skinless chicken breasts
½ head cabbage, thinly sliced, or 2 zucchini, thinly sliced lengthwise
1 tablespoon vegetable oil
1 pound Chinese egg noodles or regular spaghetti

*M*ix together the tahini or sesame paste and peanut butter in a large bowl. Gradually add water and stir until smooth. Add the chili oil, sugar, soy sauce, ½ cup sesame oil, garlic, and vinegar. Whisk until smooth. Season to taste with ground pepper. In a large pan, cover the chicken breasts with an inch or so of water. Cover and simmer until just cooked, about 10 minutes. Let cool and cut or shred into small pieces. Mix the chicken with the cabbage and vegetable oil. Cook the noodles according to package directions, toss with 1½ tablespoons sesame oil, then combine with the chicken and sauce.

Makes 4 servings

Crispy Chicken

SUSAN BLAKELY, ACTRESS

1 whole chicken, cut into pieces
1 tablespoon coarse kosher salt
1 tablespoon black pepper
1 teaspoon lemon pepper
1 teaspoon ground ginger
1 teaspoon garlic powder
1 teaspoon paprika
1 teaspoon dried thyme

*P*reheat the oven to 375°F. Wash the chicken thoroughly and pat dry with paper towels. Using a large sheet of aluminum foil, sprinkle half the salt and pepper on the foil. Place the chicken pieces in the foil and sprinkle with remaining salt and pepper, lemon pepper, ginger, garlic powder, paprika, and thyme. Bake for 1 hour, then turn the temperature down to 350°F and continue baking for 1 hour longer. During the last ½ hour, drain off any grease or liquid, reserving 4 tablespoons. Use this to baste the chicken pieces. The chicken should bake dry for the last ½ hour.

Makes 4 servings

Microwave Crispy Coated Chicken

ZANNE SHAW, STAND-IN TO MS. LANSBURY

1 broiler or fryer chicken, quar-
tered, about 2½ to 3½ pounds
1 cup cornflake crumbs
6 tablespoons grated Parmesan
cheese
2 teaspoons parsley flakes

*S*kin the chicken pieces and remove any excess fat. In a large bowl or dish, combine the cornflake crumbs, Parmesan cheese, parsley flakes, garlic, salt, and pepper. In a separate bowl, beat the eggs and stir in the melted butter. Dip the chicken pieces in the

1 clove garlic, minced
½ teaspoon salt
Black pepper to taste
2 large eggs
¼ pound (1 stick) butter or
  margarine, melted

egg mixture, then coat in crumbs. Arrange in a single layer in a glass baking dish, bony side down and thick pieces around the outside of the dish. Cover with wax paper. The chicken should be microwaved for 5½ to 8 minutes per pound. Microwave on HIGH for half the time. Halfway through microwaving, rearrange the chicken so that the pieces that are least cooked are placed around the outside of the dish. Discard the wax paper and microwave for the remaining time.

Makes 4 servings

Chicken and Dumplings

CRAIG HEFFREN, RIGGING KEY

1½ pounds boneless, skinless
  chicken breasts
2 cups instant biscuit mix
⅔ cup milk
1 tablespoon black pepper

In a 4-quart saucepan, boil 8 cups water. Add the chicken and cook for 10 minutes. In a bowl, mix together the biscuit mix, milk, and pepper thoroughly. Form the dough into heaping spoonfuls, drop carefully into the pot with the chicken, reduce heat, and simmer for 10 minutes.

Makes 4 servings

South African Yogurt and Chicken Potjie

MUSETTA VANDER, ACTRESS

2 cups plus 2 tablespoons
   plain yogurt
2 cups plus 2 tablespoons
   dry white wine
2 teaspoons dried thyme
2 teaspoons grated lemon peel
1 large yellow onion, finely
   chopped
1 teaspoon freshly ground
   black pepper
3 bay leaves
1 teaspoon dried tarragon
4½ pounds chicken pieces
2 tablespoons vegetable oil
2 green bell peppers, chopped
1⅓ cups peeled sliced carrots
6 large potatoes, peeled and
   quartered
½ cup sliced dried apricots
1 cup sliced fresh green beans
¾ cup sliced fresh mushrooms
Salt to taste
2 ounces mushroom soup
   powder (optional)

*M*ix together the yogurt, wine, thyme, lemon peel, onion, pepper, bay leaves, and tarragon. Pour over the chicken and marinate in the refrigerator for 6 to 8 hours or overnight. Heat a three-legged potjie pot (a number 3 pot is recommended) or a large saucepan until very hot. Remove the chicken from the marinade, reserving the marinade, and fry a few pieces at a time in the oil with the bell peppers until golden brown. Reduce the heat and arrange the carrots, potatoes, apricots, green beans, and mushrooms in layers on top of the meat. Sprinkle with salt and add the reserved marinade. Replace the lid and simmer slowly for 2 hours. Should the potjie render too much liquid, it can be thickened with mushroom soup powder. Remove the chicken and vegetables, mix in the soup powder, if desired, with the sauce, and simmer for another 15 minutes. Most important: do not stir! Serve with mashed potatoes or rice and the thickened potjie sauce.

Makes 6 servings

Gourmet Chicken

SUZANNE WAITE, SCRIPT SUPERVISOR

8 tablespoons (1 stick) butter
  or margarine
¼ cup oil
6 whole chicken breasts, skinned
  and boned
1½ cups chopped carrot
2 medium yellow onions,
  roughly chopped
2 cups Sauternes wine
2 teaspoons garlic salt
1 teaspoon celery salt
½ teaspoon dried thyme
½ teaspoon black pepper
2 cups milk
¼ cup flour
½ cup slivered almonds
  (optional)

Heat 4 tablespoons butter and the oil in a skillet. Fry the chicken until golden brown. Drain and set aside. Place the carrot, onions, wine, and spices in a blender and liquefy. Return the chicken and the blended mixture to the skillet. Cover and simmer for ½ hour. Remove the chicken and keep warm in the oven. Soften the remaining 4 tablespoons butter. Place the sauce from the skillet, the milk, softened butter, and flour into the blender and blend until smooth. Pour into the skillet and cook over medium heat until thickened, stirring constantly. Serve the chicken on a bed of rice, topped with the sauce. Garnish with slivered almonds, if desired.

Makes 6 servings

Healthy Cornmeal Breaded Chicken

MARY FLEMING, SET COSTUMER FOR MS. LANSBURY

1 chicken, cut into pieces,
  about 2 pounds
¼ cup cornmeal
¼ cup whole wheat flour
¼ teaspoon dried oregano
¼ teaspoon dried marjoram
Black pepper to taste
1 egg white, lightly beaten

*P*reheat the oven to 350°F. Remove the skin and any fat from the chicken. Combine the cornmeal, flour, oregano, marjoram, and pepper. Dip each piece of chicken in the egg white, then roll in the cornmeal mix. Bake, uncovered, in a shallow pan for 1 hour.

Makes 4 servings

Herb-Flavored Roast Chicken

CAROL LUPO, WARDROBE

1 large shallot, finely chopped
3 tablespoons chopped fresh
  parsley
3 tablespoons chopped fresh dill
1½ teaspoons crushed dried
  rosemary
½ teaspoon crushed dried thyme
3 tablespoons corn oil
¼ cup cider vinegar
Cayenne pepper to taste
1 broiling chicken, about 3 pounds

*C*ombine all ingredients except the chicken in a large bowl. Blend well to make a marinade. Place the chicken on its back. Lift, but do not remove the skin by gently pushing your finger under the breast skin and then to the thigh and leg. Gently spoon some of the marinade under the skin as far as it will go. Press the skin down and skewer in place. With a sharp-pronged fork, prick the skin of the wings and back and spoon in some of the marinade, reserving the rest. Turn to coat. Cover with aluminum foil and refrigerate overnight. Remove from the refrigerator and

foil and let sit out 1 hour before roasting.

Preheat the oven to 350°F. Place the bird on a rack in a roasting pan. Pour half the marinade over the bird. Roast, uncovered, for ½ hour. Pour the rest of the marinade over the bird and roast for an additional 45 minutes. Remove from the oven and loosely cover with waxed paper. Let stand for 5 minutes before carving. This marinade is delicious for veal and pork chops as well.

Makes 4 to 6 servings

Low-Calorie Chicken Cacciatore

MICHAEL HELGESEN, DRIVER CAPTAIN

1 chicken, about 3½ pounds
1 tablespoon olive oil
1 can (14 ounces) tomato paste
6 large tomatoes, cored and diced
1 large red onion, cut into strips
1 red bell pepper, cut into strips
1 yellow bell pepper, cut into strips
1 green bell pepper, cut into strips
3 cloves garlic, minced
Salt and black pepper to taste
½ teaspoon dried oregano
½ teaspoon dried thyme
⅓ cup chopped parsley or cilantro

Cut the chicken into pieces and boil in water for 10 to 15 minutes. Remove from heat, drain, and remove the skin. Heat the olive oil in a large saucepan over moderate heat. Coat the chicken with half the tomato paste and braise in the hot oil, turning frequently, until its color changes. Add the tomatoes. Add the remaining tomato paste. Add the onion, peppers, and garlic and stir. Add the salt, pepper, oregano, and thyme and stir well. Add the parsley or cilantro and stir well. Cover and simmer for 1½ to 2 hours, stirring frequently, until the chicken is tender. Serve over pasta or rice.

Makes 4 servings

Mexican Chicken

DANA CROCKER, TRANSPORTATION CAPTAIN

4 skinless chicken breasts
Salt and black pepper to taste
1 can (10¾ ounces) cream of
  mushroom soup, undiluted
1 can (10¾ ounces) cream of
  chicken soup, undiluted
1 cup milk
1 can (7 ounces) green chili salsa
1 yellow onion, grated
8 corn tortillas
¾ pound Cheddar cheese, shredded

Preheat the oven to 350°F. Lightly season the chicken with salt and pepper and wrap in foil. Bake for 1 hour. Let the chicken cool, then remove the bones. In a mixing bowl, mix together the soups, milk, salsa, and grated onion. Cut the tortillas into 1-inch strips. Oil an 8 by 13-inch ovenproof dish and layer in the tortillas, chicken, and soup mixture. Top with cheese. Chill for 2 to 3 hours or overnight. Preheat the oven to 325°F. Bake for 1¼ hours.

Makes 6 servings

Mexican Chicken Tofu

SUZANNE WAITE, SCRIPT SUPERVISOR

1 package (14 ounces) firm tofu,
  drained well and cubed
2 jars (7 ounces each) mild salsa
1 cup sliced fresh scallions
1 cup fresh or frozen corn kernels
  (if frozen, do not precook)
6 half chicken breasts, skinned
  and boned

Preheat the oven to 375°F. Sprinkle the tofu on the bottom of an oiled casserole or baking dish. Pour half the salsa over it. Sprinkle half the scallions and all the corn over the tofu. Place the chicken breasts over the tofu and vegetables. Sprinkle the remaining scallions over the chicken and add the remaining salsa. Bake for 40 minutes, or until the chicken is tender and the casserole is very hot and bubbly.

Makes 6 servings

Orange and Cilantro Chicken

CHERÉ RAE, STUNT DOUBLE TO MS. LANSBURY

1 roasting chicken, about 3 pounds
1 clove garlic, halved
1 cup chopped cilantro, rinsed
1 cup fresh orange juice
1 orange, cut into wedges

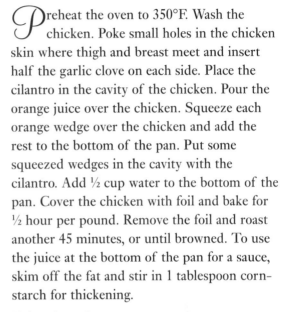

Preheat the oven to 350°F. Wash the chicken. Poke small holes in the chicken skin where thigh and breast meet and insert half the garlic clove on each side. Place the cilantro in the cavity of the chicken. Pour the orange juice over the chicken. Squeeze each orange wedge over the chicken and add the rest to the bottom of the pan. Put some squeezed wedges in the cavity with the cilantro. Add ½ cup water to the bottom of the pan. Cover the chicken with foil and bake for ½ hour per pound. Remove the foil and roast another 45 minutes, or until browned. To use the juice at the bottom of the pan for a sauce, skim off the fat and stir in 1 tablespoon cornstarch for thickening.

Makes 6 servings

The Case of the Scarlet Chicken

DEVEON SHUDIC, SPECIAL EFFECTS

2 chicken breasts
1 tablespoon olive oil
Garlic powder to taste
Salt and coarsely ground black
 pepper to taste
1 jar (7 ounces) salsa

Wash the chicken breasts and pat dry with paper towels. Over medium-high heat, brown the chicken in the olive oil. Season with garlic powder, salt, and pepper. Reduce the heat to medium and cover the pan. Cook for 12 more minutes, then reduce the heat to low and pour the salsa evenly over the chicken breasts. Cover and simmer for 5 to 10 minutes longer.

Makes 2 servings

South American Spicy Chicken and Pumpkin Stew

SHANNON LITTEN, WOMEN'S WARDROBE SUPERVISOR

1 pound chicken breasts, skinned,
 boned, and cubed
6 ounces chicken thighs, skinned,
 boned, and cubed
½ cup chopped yellow onion
3 cups cubed, peeled pumpkin
1½ cups peeled, cubed red potatoes
1 cup low-sodium chicken broth
½ cup Chablis or other dry white
 wine

Coat a large Dutch oven with cooking spray and place over medium-high heat until hot. Add the chicken and onion and sauté for 4 minutes, or until the chicken loses its pink color. Add the pumpkin, potatoes, chicken broth, wine, peppers, curry powder, ginger, salt, cumin, nutmeg, and garlic. Bring to a boil. Cover, reduce heat, and simmer for 25 minutes or until the vegetables are tender.

2 tablespoons diced serrano or
  jalapeño peppers
1 teaspoon curry powder
1 teaspoon grated peeled fresh
  ginger root
½ teaspoon salt
¼ teaspoon ground cumin
Ground nutmeg to taste
3 cloves garlic, minced
¼ cup water
1 tablespoon cornstarch

Combine the water and cornstarch. Stir well
and add to the pan. Bring to a boil and cook
for 1 minute, stirring constantly.

Makes 4 servings

Southern Fried Chicken

CASSIE YATES, ACTRESS

2 cups flour
1 teaspoon salt
½ teaspoon black pepper
½ teaspoon dried oregano
Cayenne pepper to taste
1 large egg
1 cup milk
1 whole fryer chicken,
  cut into pieces
2 tablespoons vegetable oil

*I*n a brown paper bag, combine the flour,
salt, pepper, oregano, and cayenne pepper. Whisk the egg and milk together. Coat the
chicken in the milk and egg mixture and then
place it in the flour bag. Shake well. Heat the
oil in a skillet over medium heat. When the oil
is sizzling, add the chicken and cook until
crispy and golden brown.

Makes 4 servings

The Spicy Lemon Chicken Caper

LISA DARR, ACTRESS

1½ cups flour
1 teaspoon salt
1 teaspoon dried tarragon
1 teaspoon cayenne pepper
1 teaspoon dried oregano
1 teaspoon black pepper
4 boneless, skinless chicken breasts
Juice of 5 lemons
2 tablespoons butter
1 jar (6 ounces) capers, drained
1 pound pasta, any type

*C*ombine the flour, salt, tarragon, cayenne pepper, oregano, and black pepper in a shallow dish. Soak the chicken for 10 to 15 minutes in the lemon juice, then dredge in the flour mixture. Melt the butter in a skillet and add the capers. Fry the chicken thoroughly and keep warm in the oven. Boil the pasta, drain, then fry briefly in the remaining butter and capers, adding additional lemon juice as desired. Top the pasta with the chicken.

Makes 4 servings

Spinach and Chicken Enchiladas

BRETT PORTER, ACTOR

2 large eggs, beaten
1 cup chopped, cooked chicken
¼ cup heavy cream
3 cloves garlic, minced
4 tablespoons hot or mild salsa
1 cup shredded Monterey Jack cheese
⅓ cup grated Parmesan cheese
6 flour tortillas

*I*n a large saucepan, combine the eggs, chicken, cream, garlic, salsa, Monterey Jack, and Parmesan cheese. Cook over low heat until the cheeses melt. Spread this mix-

1 large tomato, cored and diced

1 pound fresh spinach, cooked
and drained

1 can (7 ounces) green chili salsa

1 cup shredded Cheddar cheese

½ cup sour cream

3 scallions, sliced

ture on the tortillas, and layer with tomato and spinach. Roll up and place in a baking dish. Top with green chili salsa and Cheddar cheese. Broil for 5 to 10 minutes. Top with sour cream and scallions.

Makes 6 servings

Thai Peanut Wok

PAUL LINKE, ACTOR

2 skinless chicken breasts, sliced
into 2-inch strips

⅓ cup soy sauce

6 tablespoons olive oil

1 medium yellow onion, diced

1 pound fresh French-cut
green beans

1 can (14 ounces) whole kernel
corn, drained, or 4 ears of fresh
corn cut from the cob

4 cups bean sprouts (optional)

2 cups Thai peanut sauce

Heat a wok over high heat for 5 minutes. Add the chicken and ½ cup water. Stir, cover, and cook for 5 minutes. Add the soy sauce and cook for another 2 minutes. Remove the chicken and any liquid and set aside. Wipe the wok clean with paper towels, and return to the burner. Increase heat to high. Add the olive oil. When the wok is hot, add the onion. Cook, stirring, until the onion is translucent. Add the green beans. Stir, cover, and cook for another 5 minutes, until the vegetables feel firm, not mushy. Add the corn. Stir, cover, and cook for 4 to 5 minutes more. Add the chicken and cooking broth. Stir, cover, and cook for another 2 minutes. Add the bean sprouts, if using. Stir, cover, and cook for 2 minutes more. Serve over rice with Thai peanut sauce.

Makes 4 servings

Chicken and Wild Rice

JUDITH LYTLE, ACTRESS

3 chicken breasts with bones
½ cup sherry
1 yellow onion, cut into large
 sections
1 box (6 ounces) wild rice
½ pound fresh mushrooms, sliced
1 tablespoon butter
½ pint sour cream
1 can (10¾ ounces) cream of
 mushroom soup, undiluted

*P*lace the chicken, sherry, and enough water to cover the chicken in a large saucepan and bring to a boil. Add the onion, cover tightly, and boil gently for 20 minutes, or until the chicken is tender. Let cool. Remove the chicken, reserving any liquid. Skin and bone the chicken, and cut into bite-size pieces. Preheat the oven to 350°F. Prepare the wild rice according to package instructions, using the reserved broth in place of the liquid called for. Sauté the mushrooms in the butter. In a large casserole dish, combine the rice, chicken, and mushrooms with the sour cream and cream of mushroom soup. Cover and bake for ½ hour. This casserole improves with age and can be prepared a day ahead of time and refrigerated.

Makes 4 servings

Chicken Mole

DANA CROCKER, TRANSPORTATION CAPTAIN

1 chicken, cleaned, deboned,
 giblets discarded, and cut
 into pieces
1 tablespoon shortening

*B*oil the chicken pieces in lightly salted water until done. Set aside. In a large skillet, melt the shortening over low heat until liquefied but not hot. Add the peanut butter

2 tablespoons creamy peanut butter
1 can (3 ounces) La Victoria mole
  (available from Mexican or
  Cuban markets)
1 can (28 ounces) red chili sauce

and stir until creamy. Add ½ to ¾ can of mole, as preferred. Add the chili sauce and simmer over low heat for ½ hour. If the sauce gets too thick, add a little broth from the cooked chicken. Add the chicken and simmer for 1 hour.

Makes 4 servings

Turkey Loaf

BRUCE GRAY, ACTOR

1 can (14½ ounces) chicken broth
1 package (1¼ ounces) onion soup
  mix
2 large eggs, beaten
1 package (6 ounces) seasoned
  instant stuffing mix
1½ pounds ground turkey
3 tablespoons apricot jam, peach
  jam, or marmalade
1 tablespoon hot mustard

*P*reheat the oven to 350°F. In a medium bowl, combine the chicken broth, onion soup mix, eggs, and stuffing mix. Let sit for 5 minutes, until thickened. Add the ground turkey and mix thoroughly. Shape into a loaf and place in a greased loaf pan. Bake for 1 hour. While the loaf cooks, mix together the jam, mustard, and 1 tablespoon water in a heat-resistant bowl and microwave on HIGH until bubbly. Remove the loaf from the oven and glaze with the jam mixture. Return the loaf to the oven for 15 minutes. Remove and let sit for 15 minutes before serving.

Makes 4 servings

Turkey-Spinach Meat Loaf

DAVID SCOTT, PROP MAN

1 pound ground turkey
½ pound spinach, chopped
½ cup chopped fresh basil
½ cup grated carrots
½ cup chopped onion
3 medium eggs
½ cup tomato purée
½ cup dry breadcrumbs or
* wheat germ*
½ teaspoon salt
½ teaspoon black pepper

Preheat the oven to 375°F. Mix together the turkey, spinach, basil, carrots, onion, eggs, and tomato purée. Add the breadcrumbs, salt, and pepper and mix well. Spray an 8 by 4-inch loaf pan with cooking spray. Gently fold the meat into the pan: do not pack densely. Bake for 40 to 50 minutes. Cool, then remove from pan.

Makes 8 servings

Italian-Style Baked Rabbit with Wine and Garlic

JOE RIZZO, CONSTRUCTION FOREMAN

1 rabbit, cut into pieces
¼ cup plus 3 tablespoons olive oil
½ cup red wine
6 potatoes, peeled and quartered
1 yellow onion, finely chopped
Salt and black pepper to taste
1½ tablespoons chopped fresh
* thyme*
4 pounds large tomatoes
1 cup water

Preheat the oven to 325°F. Wash the rabbit in salt water and vinegar and dry with a cloth. Lightly panfry the rabbit in ¼ cup olive oil, then place it in a large baking pan. Add the wine, potatoes, and onion and season with salt and pepper. Drizzle the remaining 3 tablespoons olive oil over the potatoes and sprinkle with thyme. Squeeze the tomatoes, seeds and all, over the rabbit. Add the water. Cover the pan with foil and bake 2 hours. During the last

1/4 cup grated Parmesan or
  Romano cheese
2 cloves garlic, minced

1/2 hour of baking, remove the foil and sprinkle with cheese and garlic. Cook, uncovered, for the remaining 1/2 hour.

Makes 4 servings

Grilled Trout in White Wine Sauce

MICHAEL HELGENSEN, DRIVER CAPTAIN

2 whole trout, cleaned
1 1/2 tablespoons olive oil
4 slices lemon, 1/8-inch thick
1 teaspoon salt
1 teaspoon black pepper
1 teaspoon dried basil
1/2 teaspoon dried sage
1/2 medium red onion, diced
1/4 cup chopped cilantro or
  fresh parsley
2 cloves garlic, minced
1 1/2 cups dry white wine

*P*repare a charcoal grill. Coat the fish with the olive oil and place in the center of a large piece of heavy aluminum foil. In the cavity of the fish, place the lemon slices. In a separate bowl, mix together the salt, pepper, basil, and sage. Add half of this to the cavity of the fish, and sprinkle the rest over the exterior. Add half the onion and half the cilantro or parsley to the cavity, and spread the rest over the fish. Do the same with the garlic. Fold the foil snugly around the fish so no liquid will escape, with the seam on top. Before you seal it completely, add the wine.

Grill over hot coals for 5 to 8 minutes. As the wine boils, the foil will expand against the long seam across the top of the pouch. Once expanded almost to the point of opening the top seal, puncture with a fork two to four times to relieve pressure. Serve over steamed rice with the juices from the foil pouch as a sauce.

Makes 4 servings

Pesco Marinata

PAUL MANTEE, ACTOR

2 pounds halibut, cut into
  2-inch chunks
2 cups flour
Salt and black pepper to taste
4 cups olive oil
6 cloves garlic, minced
3 whole dried chili peppers
1 cup chopped fresh rosemary
4 cups red wine vinegar

Dust the fish in the flour and season with salt and pepper. In a large skillet, fry the fish in ½ cup olive oil until lightly brown. Stack the fish in an uncovered Crock-Pot and let cool. In the same skillet, cook the garlic, chili peppers, and rosemary, stirring until the garlic is golden brown. Don't let it burn. Add the remaining 3½ cups olive oil and vinegar and bring to a rolling boil. Pour over the fish carefully, cover, and chill at least 24 hours. The dish will keep for at least 1 month in the refrigerator. Serve chilled. This makes a great first course.

Makes 4 servings

Haddock Pot Pie

ALLAN MILLER, ACTOR

2 medium yellow onions, sliced
2 tablespoons butter, melted
1 pound boiling potatoes, peeled
  and sliced
1 pound haddock, filleted and
  cubed
1 egg yolk, beaten
⅔ cup sour cream

Preheat the oven to 350°F. Sauté the onions in the 2 tablespoons melted butter. Grease a 1½-quart ovenproof casserole dish. Arrange the sliced potatoes, fish, and sautéed onions in alternate layers, ending with potatoes. Blend the egg yolk into the sour cream. Season with salt and pepper. Pour over the top layer of potatoes, sprinkle with the

Salt and black pepper to taste
⅓ cup dry breadcrumbs
2 tablespoons butter

breadcrumbs, and dot with the remaining butter. Bake for 35 minutes, or until the top is golden brown.

Makes 4 servings

Orange Roughy in Citrus Sauce

JENNIFER MANASSERI, ACTRESS

1 pound orange roughy fillets
¼ cup frozen orange juice concentrate
2 tablespoons lemon juice
1 teaspoon dried dill
1 teaspoon paprika
2 tablespoons minced fresh parsley
½ cup water
6 tablespoons orange marmalade
1 teaspoon arrowroot powder

*P*lace the fish in a shallow nonmetal casserole dish. Combine the orange juice concentrate, lemon juice, dill, paprika, parsley, and water and mix to dissolve the orange juice concentrate. Reserve ½ cup of this mixture for sauce, and pour the remaining mixture over the fish. Cover and marinate in the refrigerator for at least 45 minutes. Preheat the broiler. Remove the fish from the marinade and place on a broiler pan. Add 3 tablespoons marmalade to the marinade and heat. Broil the fish 4 inches from the heat source for 10 to 15 minutes or until the fish flakes, basting with marinade several times during cooking. While the fish is broiling, heat the reserved marinade in a small saucepan with the arrowroot and remaining 3 tablespoons marmalade until sauce begins to thicken. Transfer the fish to a serving dish. Pour the sauce over the fish or serve on the side. If desired, decorate the plate with fresh orange slices and sprigs of parsley or dill.

Makes 4 servings

Poached Salmon Steaks

PHIL BEESON, UTILITY SOUND TECHNICIAN

*1 teaspoon white vinegar
or lemon juice*
1 teaspoon salt
2 yellow onions, sliced
*1 tablespoon chopped fresh dill
or parsley*
5 white peppercorns
4 small salmon steaks

In a large skillet, boil 4 cups water and add the vinegar or lemon juice, salt, onions, dill or parsley, and peppercorns. Add the salmon steaks in a single layer. Bring to a boil again. Cover and simmer for 6 to 8 minutes, or until the fish flakes easily with a fork. Remove with a slotted spoon to a hot platter and serve with hollandaise sauce.

Makes 4 servings

Grilled Salmon

SAM ANDERSON, ACTOR

*2 pounds fresh salmon fillet, skin
removed*
Juice of 1 lemon
½ cup rock salt
1 cup light or dark brown sugar
Black pepper to taste
1 tablespoon olive oil

Wash the fillet in cold water and pat dry with paper towels. Rub both sides with fresh lemon juice. In an ovenproof baking dish large enough to hold the fillets flat, sprinkle a handful of rock salt (enough to look scattered but not enough to cover the entire bottom surface). Cover the salt with a layer of brown sugar. The ratio of this marinade should be 2 to 1, brown sugar to salt. Lay the fish on the rock salt and brown sugar mixture. Sprinkle the fish with the remaining rock salt and brown sugar. Season with pepper. Cover with aluminum foil and chill for 2 to 3 hours.

Heat the grill to medium-high heat and brush lightly with the olive oil. If the grill smokes a little when you brush on the oil, then you know that it is hot enough for the salmon. Remove the salmon from the marinade and run cold water over it. Note that the salt and sugar has produced a glaze on the fish that will help retain the juices. Place the fillet on the grill and cook for 3 minutes per side or slightly longer, depending upon the thickness of the fillet. The fish is cooked when it flakes and the inside is a light pink color. Remove from the grill and serve with more lemon juice, tartar sauce, or fresh papaya salsa.

Makes 4 servings

Salmon Baked in Wine and Butter

PHIL BEESON, UTILITY SOUND TECHNICIAN

1 whole salmon or 6 salmon steaks
¼ pound (1 stick) butter
2 cups white wine
½ teaspoon garlic powder
½ teaspoon onion powder
1 bay leaf
Salt and black pepper to taste
1 lemon, sliced
1 yellow onion, sliced
¼ cup chopped fresh parsley

Preheat the oven to 350°F. Line a large baking pan with foil, enough to also cover the fish loosely. Place the fish in the pan. In a small saucepan, melt the butter with the wine, garlic powder, onion powder, and bay leaf. Season with salt and pepper. Pour the sauce over the fish. Arrange the lemon slices and onion slices over the fish and sprinkle with parsley. Seal the foil and bake for 45 minutes to 1 hour.

Makes 6 servings

Seared Ahi Tuna with Wasabi Cream Sauce

LISA AKEY AND RAPHAEL SBARGE, ACTORS

2 cloves garlic, minced
4 tablespoons olive oil
⅓ cup wasabi (found in
  Asian supermarkets)
¼ cup cognac
1½ cups heavy cream
¼ cup chicken stock
4 medium shallots, thinly sliced
1 cup flour
2 tablespoons cooking oil
4 sashimi-grade ahi (yellowfin)
  tuna fillets
¼ cup chopped fresh parsley

Sauté the garlic in 2 tablespoons of the olive oil over medium heat for 2 to 3 minutes or until slightly golden. Add the wasabi and mix thoroughly. Reduce the heat to low, add the cognac and mix thoroughly. Add the cream and chicken stock. Keep the sauce warm on top of the stove but do not boil. Place the shallots in a brown paper or Ziploc bag with the flour. Shake until the shallots are firmly coated with flour and the rings are separated. Fry them in the cooking oil until golden brown and set aside. Brush the tuna fillets on both sides with the remaining 2 tablespoons olive oil. Broil on each side for 3 to 4 minutes, or until rare or medium rare, depending on your taste. Place the seared tuna on a plate and pour the warmed wasabi cream over each fillet. Garnish with the fried shallots and parsley.

Makes 2 servings

Crab Imperial

BRYAN RODGERS, PROP MASTER

½ green bell pepper, chopped
1 tablespoon butter or margarine
1 pound crabmeat or imitation
  crabmeat
3 heaping tablespoons mayonnaise
1 teaspoon Worcestershire sauce
1 teaspoon salt

Preheat the oven to 400°F. In a skillet over medium-high heat, cook the green pepper in the butter for 1 minute. Place the cooked peppers in a mixing bowl and combine with the crabmeat, mayonnaise, Worcestershire sauce, and salt. Mix thoroughly. Spread the mixture into a baking dish and bake ½ hour or until browned on top. Serve over rice.

Makes 4 servings

Coquille St. Jacques (Scallops and Mushrooms in Cream Sauce)

PAUL CONTI, COMPUTER GRAPHICS

1 pound bay scallops
¼ pound wild mushrooms, chopped
2 cloves garlic, minced
⅓ cup clarified butter
Salt and black pepper to taste
⅓ cup white wine
⅓ cup heavy cream
½ tablespoon chopped parsley
Lemon wedges to garnish

In a saucepan, sauté the scallops, mushrooms, and garlic in the clarified butter. Season with salt and pepper. Slowly stir in the wine, a few tablespoons at a time. When the scallops are almost done, about 3 minutes, add the cream. Allow the mixture to bubble for about 2 minutes, until it reduces to a thick consistency. Total cooking time for the scallops should be about 5 minutes. Garnish with parsley and lemon wedges. Serve over pasta or with hot, crusty sourdough bread.

Makes 4 servings

Sherried Scallops

BETTY ABBOTT-GRIFFIN, SCRIPT SUPERVISOR

1/4 cup flour
1/2 teaspoon seasoned salt
1 pound scallops, washed
 and well drained
2 tablespoons butter
1/3 cup dry sherry
1/4 teaspoon dried tarragon

*I*n a mixing bowl, combine the flour and salt. Toss the scallops in the flour and salt mixture and shake off excess. In a skillet, melt the butter. Add the scallops, sherry, and tarragon. Cook for 5 to 7 minutes. Serve over rice or pasta.

Makes 4 servings

Indian-Style Barbecued Shrimp

ERICK AVARI AND MAGGI WALKER, ACTORS

1/2 cup plus 1/4 cup olive oil
1/3 cup lemon juice
1 medium yellow onion, chopped
1 clove garlic, minced
1 square inch peeled fresh ginger,
 chopped
Hot chili peppers to taste, chopped
1 1/2 teaspoons salt
1/2 teaspoon freshly ground black
 pepper
3 pounds fresh or frozen jumbo
 shrimp, peeled, deveined, and
 butterflied

*I*n a blender or food processor, combine 1/2 cup olive oil, the lemon juice, onion, garlic, ginger, chili peppers, salt, and black pepper. Blend into a paste. Mix the shrimp into the blended paste and chill in a covered container for 1 hour. Prepare the grill. Remove the shrimp from the paste and brush the undersides of the shrimp with the remaining 1/4 cup olive oil. Place the shrimp on the grill. Brush the tops with paste and cook until they brown. Turn and repeat the process. Garnish with lemon wedges and sprigs of parsley or dill. Served with rice, peas, and green salad.

Makes 6 servings

108

Cajun Barbecued Shrimp

DAVE MARSIK, SET LIGHTING

*8 pounds large shrimp, peeled,
deveined, and washed*
½ pound (2 sticks) butter
1 jar (8 ounces) chili sauce
3 tablespoons Worcestershire sauce
3 lemons, sliced
6 cloves garlic, minced
4 tablespoons lemon juice
4 tablespoons chopped fresh parsley
2 teaspoons paprika
1 teaspoon dried oregano
2 teaspoons crushed red pepper
1 teaspoon Tabasco sauce
3 tablespoons liquid smoke
Salt and black pepper to taste

Spread the shrimp out in a large shallow baking pan. Combine all the other ingredients in a saucepan and cook over low heat until well blended. Pour the sauce over the shrimp and chill for 4 hours, basting and turning every ½ hour. Preheat the oven to 300°F. Bake for 30 to 40 minutes, turning the shrimp every 10 minutes. Serve in soup bowls with sourdough garlic bread to dip in the sauce.

Makes 8 servings

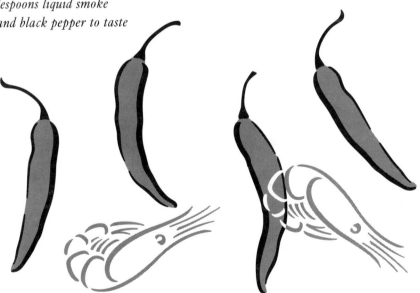

Pansit (Filipino Shrimp and Pork)

MIKE BALKER, COSTUMER

2 pounds boneless pork,
 cut into thin strips
8 cloves garlic, sliced
3 tablespoons olive oil
1 tablespoon soy sauce
2 medium yellow onions,
 finely chopped
3 cups finely chopped celery
2 tablespoons vegetable oil
1½ pounds thin spaghetti
1 pound shrimp, peeled,
 deveined, cut intobite-size
 pieces and parboiled
2 large eggs, hard-boiled
 and sliced into wedges
2 lemons, sliced into wedges
4 scallions, sliced

In a saucepan, cook the pork with ½ the sliced garlic in the olive oil until light brown. Add the soy sauce and enough water to cover the pork, and simmer until tender. In another pan, sauté the onions, celery, and remaining garlic in the vegetable oil until tender. Cook the spaghetti according to package directions: drain, rinse, and set aside. In a large pot, combine the pork, vegetables, and shrimp, including the liquids from the pork and onion mixture. Heat thoroughly. Reduce heat and simmer for 5 minutes. Pour over the spaghetti and serve garnished with the egg and lemon wedges and sprinkled with the scallions.

Makes 6 servings

Grilled Shrimp Fajitas

STEVE IRWIN, VIDEO PLAYBACK

Juice of 1 lemon
1 teaspoon dried oregano
1 teaspoon Creole seasoning
1 tablespoon chopped cilantro
1 tablespoon plus 1 teaspoon
 chopped pickled jalapeño peppers
1 teaspoon Tabasco sauce

In a large bowl, combine the lemon juice, oregano, ½ teaspoon Creole seasoning, cilantro, 1 tablespoon jalapeño peppers, Tabasco sauce, and paprika. Add the shrimp to this mixture and chill for 3 to 4 hours. Prepare the grill. In a small bowl, combine the melted

½ teaspoon paprika
2 pounds shrimp, shelled and
   deveined
¼ pound (1 stick) butter, melted
9 cloves garlic
1 red bell pepper, thinly sliced
1 onion, thinly sliced
½ tablespoon olive oil

butter and 6 cloves garlic. Skewer the shrimp and grill, basting as needed with the butter and garlic mixture. After basting, sprinkle the shrimp with the remaining ½ teaspoon Creole seasoning.

Mince the remaining 3 cloves garlic. In a skillet, lightly sauté the red pepper, onion, remaining 1 teaspoon jalapeño peppers, and minced garlic in the oil. Toss the shrimp and vegetables together and serve with flour tortillas and salsa.

Makes 4 servings

Shrimp Scampi

SUSAN BLAKELY, ACTRESS

2 tablespoons olive oil
2 pounds shrimp, peeled, deveined,
   and washed in cold water
½ cup vermouth or Chablis wine
½ teaspoon salt
1 teaspoon grated Parmesan
   cheese
½ teaspoon chopped parsley
3 cloves garlic, minced
¼ cup chopped yellow onion
¼ pound mushrooms, chopped

*H*eat the olive oil in a large skillet. Add the shrimp, vermouth or Chablis, salt, Parmesan cheese, parsley, garlic, and onion. Cook the shrimp for 1½ minutes on each side. Add the mushrooms just before the shrimp are done.

Makes 4 servings

Sausage Quiche

BRYAN MOSS, WARDROBE

8 spicy or mild sausage links
½ yellow onion, chopped
½ green bell pepper, chopped
3 cloves garlic, minced
1 tablespoon flour
2 cups shredded cheese, any type
1 prebaked deep-dish piecrust
4 large eggs
1½ cups evaporated milk
1 tablespoon chopped fresh parsley
¾ teaspoon salt
¼ teaspoon black pepper

Preheat the oven to 375°F. Fry the sausage in a skillet until done. Remove from the pan and drain on paper towels. Sauté the onion, green pepper, and garlic for 3 to 4 minutes. In a mixing bowl, combine the flour and 1½ cups of the cheese. Crumble in the cooked sausage. Add the pepper and onion mixture. Mix gently and spread on the bottom of the prebaked piecrust. In a separate bowl, whisk together the eggs, evaporated milk, parsley, salt, and pepper. Pour into the piecrust, covering the filling. Top with the remaining ½ cup cheese. Bake for 35 to 40 minutes, or until the filling is set.

Makes 6 servings

Spinach Quiche

VINCE MCEVEETY, DIRECTOR

½ yellow onion, chopped
1 tablespoon butter
1 package (10 ounces) chopped
 frozen spinach
6 large eggs
¼ teaspoon dried basil
1 teaspoon Tabasco sauce

Preheat the oven to 350°F. Sauté the onion in the butter until translucent. Add the frozen spinach and simmer until the spinach is just defrosted. Combine the eggs, basil, Tabasco sauce, and whipping cream and blend together without whipping. In a separate bowl, mix together the cheeses. Line each

1 cup whipping cream
¾ pound Monterey Jack cheese, shredded
¾ pound sharp Cheddar cheese, shredded
2 prebaked deep-dish piecrusts
Paprika to taste

piecrust with ¼ of the cheese mixture. Add the remaining cheese to the egg mixture and divide the cheese and egg mixture evenly into each piecrust. Sprinkle with paprika and bake 40 minutes. These quiches freeze well.

Makes 12 servings

Beef Nacho Casserole

ZANNE SHAW, STAND-IN TO MS. LANSBURY

1 pound ground beef
1 jar (12 ounces) chunky salsa
1 can (15 ounces) corn kernels
¾ cup mayonnaise
1 tablespoon chili powder
2 cups crushed tortilla chips
2 cups shredded sharp Cheddar cheese or Monterey Jack cheese

Preheat the oven to 350°F. In a skillet, brown the ground beef. Drain the beef, then stir in the salsa, corn, mayonnaise, and chili powder. Layer half the meat mixture into a greased 9 by 12-inch pan, followed by a layer of chips and a layer of cheese. Repeat another layer of meat, chips, and cheese. Bake for 20 minutes, or until heated through.

Makes 6 servings

Chili Corn Casserole

MARK ROEMER, LOCATION MAN

1 can (17 ounces) creamed corn
1 can (4 ounces) diced green chilies
1 jar (4 ounces) diced pimientos, drained
¼ pound (1 stick) butter, melted
2 large eggs, beaten
½ cup cornmeal
½ teaspoon salt
1 cup sour cream
2 cups shredded Monterey Jack cheese

*P*reheat the oven to 375°F. Mix together all the ingredients in a large bowl. Turn into a buttered shallow 1½-quart baking dish. Bake, uncovered, for 40 minutes, or until set.

Makes 4 servings

Never-Fail Cheese Soufflé

ZANNE SHAW, STAND-IN TO MS. LANSBURY

¼ pound (1 stick) butter or margarine, softened
10 slices white bread
¾ pound sharp Cheddar cheese, shredded
¾ pound mozzarella cheese, shredded
8 large eggs, lightly beaten
3 cups half-and-half
¼ teaspoon paprika
½ teaspoon onion powder
½ teaspoon curry powder

*B*utter a large, shallow, rectangular baking dish or 2 square baking dishes. Remove the crusts from the bread, butter each slice, and cut into cubes. Place half the cubes in the baking dish and sprinkle with half the Cheddar and mozzarella cheeses, then add the remaining bread cubes in another layer and top with remaining cheeses. Combine the eggs, half-and-half, paprika, onion powder, curry powder, cayenne pepper, Worcestershire sauce and mustard, and pour over the bread and cheese. Cover and chill overnight. Preheat the oven to 325°F. Bake for 1 hour, or until a knife

⅛ teaspoon cayenne pepper
1 teaspoon Worcestershire sauce
1 teaspoon dry mustard

inserted in the center comes out clean and the top is lightly browned.

Makes 6 servings

Cottage Pie

ANGELA LANSBURY, ACTRESS

4 pounds lean ground beef
8 tablespoons (1 stick) unsalted butter
2 medium onions, finely chopped (about ¾ pound)
4 carrots, finely chopped
3 medium leeks, finely chopped
3 stalks celery, finely chopped
¾ cup chicken broth
1 cup tomato purée
Salt and freshly ground black pepper to taste
1½ cups green peas (about 10 ounces)
8 medium potatoes, peeled
½ cup milk
½ cup heavy cream
Freshly grated nutmeg to taste

Preheat the oven to 350°F. In a large skillet over high heat, sauté the ground beef, breaking up the pieces with a wooden spoon, until it loses its raw appearance. Drain and set aside. In a large pot over low heat, melt 2 tablespoons of the butter. Add the onions, carrots, leeks, and celery and cook, covered, for 20 minutes, stirring occasionally. Do not brown. Stir in the beef, chicken broth, and tomato purée. Season with salt and pepper. Pour the mixture into a 17 by 11 by 2-inch baking dish and bake for 15 minutes, stirring occasionally. Remove from the oven and stir in the peas.

Meanwhile, cook the potatoes in lightly salted water for 20 minutes, or until soft. Mash the potatoes or press them through a food mill. Stir in the milk and cream to get a creamy consistency. Stir in the remaining butter and season with salt, pepper, and nutmeg. Spread the mashed potatoes on top of the meat. Using a fork, draw a crisscross pattern on top of the mashed potatoes. Bake in the oven for 35 to 45 minutes, or until the cottage pie is golden and bubbly. Serve immediately.

Makes 8 servings

Creamy Celery Casserole

MOE ALTAMIRANO, STUDIO GRIP

1 pound celery, cut into 1½-inch pieces (about 4 cups)
1 tablespoon butter
3 tablespoons flour
¾ cup chicken broth
¼ cup milk
Salt to taste
½ cup shredded medium sharp Cheddar cheese, shredded
½ cup sliced, blanched almonds

Bring a 6-quart pot of salted water to a boil. Add the celery and cook for 6 to 8 minutes, until it's tender but firm. Drain and set aside. Melt the butter in a saucepan and stir in the flour. Cook over medium heat for 2 minutes, stirring constantly. Slowly stir in the chicken broth and continue to cook, stirring until the sauce thickens. Add the milk and season with salt. Cook until smooth and well blended. Add the cheese and stir until melted. Add the almonds. Pour over the celery and serve immediately, or pour into a buttered casserole dish and bake at 375°F for 20 minutes, or until heated through.

Makes 4 servings

Exquisite-Yet-Simple Green Bean Casserole

KATHRYN CRESSIDA, ACTRESS

2 cans (14½ ounces each) French-
cut green beans, drained
1 can (10¾ ounces) cream of
mushroom soup, undiluted
1 can (8 ounces) sliced
water chestnuts
2 cans (6 ounces each) Durkee's
French-fried onion rings

Preheat the oven to 375°F. Combine the green beans, soup, water chestnuts, and half of the onion rings in a casserole dish. Bake for 20 minutes. Sprinkle the remaining onion rings over the casserole and bake for an additional 5 minutes. Serve hot.

Makes 6 servings

Squash Casserole

REBECCA CROSS, ACTRESS

1 cup chicken mushroom soup,
undiluted
1 jar (4 ounces) pimientos, diced
½ pint sour cream
2 yellow onions, finely chopped
1 package (2 ounces) Pepperidge
Farm Herb Seasoned
stuffing mix
1 tablespoon butter, melted
Salt and black pepper to taste
2 cups sliced yellow summer
squash

Preheat the oven to 350°F. Mix together the soup, pimientos, sour cream, onions, stuffing, and melted butter. Season with salt and pepper. Layer half of this mixture into the bottom of an ovenproof casserole dish. Spoon in the squash and layer the remaining mixture on top. Bake for 30 to 40 minutes.

Makes 4 servings

Cajun Red Beans and Rice

LOUIS HERTHUM, ACTOR

1 pound dried kidney beans
1 large yellow onion, chopped
1 stalk celery, chopped
1 large green bell pepper, chopped
4 cloves garlic, minced
1½ pounds smoked sausage
¾ cup shredded smoked pork or
  beef (optional)
1 can (28 ounces) Rotel's tomatoes
  and chili peppers (may substitute
  another brand)
Salt and black pepper to taste

Wash the beans and soak them in water for at least 8 hours or overnight. Drain and place the beans in a large pot. Add 6½ cups water, the onion, celery, bell pepper, and garlic. Cover and bring to a boil. Reduce the heat and cook over medium-low heat for 1 hour, stirring periodically to prevent sticking. While the beans are cooking, slice the sausage into bite-size pieces and brown in a skillet. Drain the sausage and add to the beans. Add the smoked meat, if using. Mash the undrained tomatoes and chilies into the beans. Season with salt and pepper. Cook until the beans are very tender and the gravy is slightly thick, about ½ hour. Serve over white rice.

Makes 6 servings

Cuban Black Beans

MARIA CANALS, ACTRESS

1 pound dried black beans
2 bay leaves
1 green bell pepper, chopped
1 medium yellow onion, chopped
4 cloves garlic, minced
1 teaspoon dried oregano
1 teaspoon ground cumin

Wash and drain the beans. Place in a large pot and cover with water. Add the bay leaves and soak overnight. Simmer over medium-low heat for 1 hour, or until the beans are soft, adding water as necessary to keep beans covered. In a separate pan, sauté the green pepper, onion, garlic, oregano, and cumin in

¼ *cup olive oil*
1 tablespoon red wine vinegar
1 tablespoon dry red wine
Salt and black pepper to taste

the olive oil until tender, then add to the beans. Stir well, then add the vinegar, wine, salt, and pepper. Cook over medium heat for 30 to 45 minutes, or until the beans are soft but firm.

Makes 6 servings

Crock-Pot Beans

PHIL BEESON, UTILITY SOUND TECHNICIAN

1 large can (59 ounces) baked beans, drained
1 can (27 ounces) kidney beans, drained
1 pound pure cane brown sugar
1 can (7 ounces) diced green chilies or diced jalapeño peppers
2 large yellow onions, chopped
1 cup steak sauce

Place the beans in a Crock-Pot. Add the remaining ingredients. Cook on high for 4 hours, stirring often. This dish is best when cooked the day before and chilled. Serve with crusty French bread.

Makes 20 servings

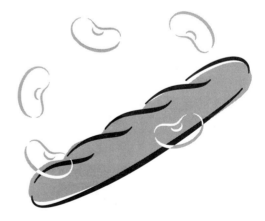

Ham Hocks and Lima Beans

TOM CULVER, WARDROBE

1 pound large or small dried
  lima beans
1 ham bone with a good amount
  of ham on it, or 3 to 4 meaty
  ham hocks
1 large white onion, sliced
Freshly ground black pepper to
  taste

*S*oak the beans in water overnight to soften. Rinse and place in a Crock-Pot. Add water to cover. Remove any excess fat from the ham bone or hocks, and add the ham and onion to the Crock-Pot. Season with pepper. (The ham is usually salty enough so that no extra salt is needed.) Cook overnight over medium heat. Remove the ham hocks and debone. Return the meat to the pot and heat through. Serve with crusty bread.

Makes 4 servings

Steak and Chili

JOHN T. TRAJILLO, GRIP

1 can (28 ounces) whole tomatoes
1½ cloves garlic, minced
1 tablespoon salt
4 cans (7 ounces each) diced green
  chilies
1 to 2 jalapeño peppers, seeded
  and diced
1½ to 2 pounds center-cut chuck
  steak, cut into 1-inch cubes

*I*n a large mixing bowl, mix together the tomatoes, garlic, salt, chilies, and jalapeño peppers to taste. Blend by crushing the tomatoes by hand and mixing well. Set aside. In a large skillet, cook the steak over medium-high heat until browned on all sides. Add the tomato mixture and simmer over low heat for 20 minutes to ½ hour.

Makes 6 servings

Quick Chili

JAMES R. WEIS, SECOND DGA

1 pound ground beef
1 can (16 ounces) kidney beans,
  drained
1 can (10¾ ounces) tomato soup,
  undiluted
⅓ cup water
1 tablespoon chili powder
¼ teaspoon black pepper
1 cup chopped yellow onion
¼ cup chopped green bell pepper

*I*n a large pot or Dutch oven, brown the beef, drain, and set aside. Add all the other ingredients and bring to a boil. Simmer for 10 minutes. Add the beef and simmer another 10 minutes.

Makes 6 servings

Spicy Black Beans

JULIA CAMPBELL, ACTRESS

¾ cup olive oil
3 cups diced red onions
10 cloves garlic, minced
2 pounds dried black beans,
  washed, soaked overnight, and
  drained
9 cups vegetable or chicken stock
3 tablespoons ground cumin
4 bay leaves
1 tablespoon dried oregano
½ teaspoon salt
¼ teaspoon cayenne pepper
½ cup chopped fresh parsley
¼ cup dry red wine
1 tablespoon lemon juice

*I*n a large pot, heat the olive oil and sauté the onions and garlic until tender. Add the beans, stock, cumin, bay leaves, oregano, salt, cayenne pepper, and parsley. Bring to a boil, reduce heat, and simmer for 2 hours. Stir in the wine and lemon juice and simmer for another ½ hour. Serve over warmed tortillas or with brown rice.

Makes 8 servings

121

Vegetable Chili

ROBERT DESIDERIO AND JUDITH LIGHT, ACTORS

¾ cup olive oil
2 yellow onions, chopped
8 cloves garlic, minced
2 red bell peppers, chopped
3 stalks celery, chopped
3 carrots, chopped
1 can (28 ounces) Italian
  peeled tomatoes
2 tablespoons chili powder
1 tablespoon ground cumin
1 tablespoon dried basil
1 tablespoon dried oregano
2 teaspoons black pepper
Salt to taste
1 teaspoon fennel seeds
2 cans (16 ounces each) dark red
  kidney beans, drained
2 tablespoons molasses
1 cup beer (nonalcoholic is
  acceptable)

Heat the olive oil in a large, deep skillet. Add the onions and garlic and sauté until translucent. Add the bell peppers, celery, and carrots and sauté for 10 minutes. Add the tomatoes with their juice, chili powder, cumin, basil, oregano, black pepper, salt, and fennel. Cook, uncovered, over medium heat for 20 minutes, stirring occasionally. Add the beans, molasses, and beer and cook for another 15 minutes. Stir. Serve in bowls with sour cream and shredded Cheddar cheese.

Makes 4 servings

Six

Pasta and Rice

"Dining in Cabot Cove with Jessica Fletcher and the Murder, She Wrote *family was always one of my favorite television acting assignments, like going home again to see old friends. One of the tastiest parts was being greeted ever so graciously by the twinkle-eyed Ms. Lansbury. Even when I was the 'dropping body' I couldn't imagine a better place to meet my end."*

—*Katherine Cannon, actress*

Baked Macaroni

PETER COIRO, SPECIAL EFFECTS

2 pounds macaroni

1 teaspoon olive oil plus
 extra for greasing

2 jars (32 ounces each)
 tomato sauce

8 cloves garlic, minced

¼ cup grated Romano cheese

2 tablespoons chopped fresh
 oregano

1½ pounds ricotta cheese

3 cups chopped broccoli

1 teaspoon honey

1 pound mozzarella
 cheese, shredded

Boil water with 1 teaspoon olive oil and cook the macaroni until al dente. Drain and set aside. Preheat the oven to 400°F. In a saucepan, combine the tomato sauce, garlic, Romano cheese, and oregano. Simmer for 15 minutes or until the cheese is melted. In a bowl, combine the ricotta cheese, broccoli, and honey. Grease the bottom of a baking dish with olive oil. Ladle the tomato sauce mixture evenly on the bottom of the dish. Cover with a layer of half the macaroni, half the ricotta cheese mixture, half the tomato sauce mixture, and half the mozzarella cheese. Repeat layers with the remaining macaroni, ricotta cheese mixture, tomato sauce mixture, and mozzarella cheese. Bake for 35 to 40 minutes.

Makes 8 servings

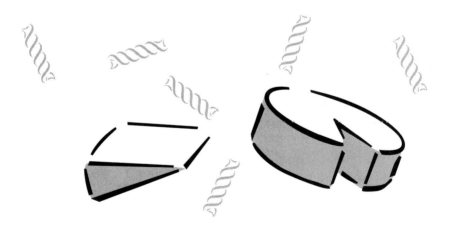

Cabot Cove Carbonara

TODD LONDON, CO-PRODUCER

5 strips bacon
½ cup olive oil
4 cloves garlic, minced
1 tomato, chopped
1 pound spaghetti or pasta of your choice
1 large egg, beaten
¼ cup grated Romano cheese

Cut the bacon into 1-inch-square pieces and cook in a skillet. Drain on paper towels and discard the grease. Add the olive oil and garlic to the same skillet and simmer for 5 minutes. Add the chopped tomato and simmer for 2 more minutes, stirring occasionally. Meanwhile, boil water and cook the spaghetti or other pasta until al dente. Drain and return to the pot. To the tomato mixture, add the egg, cheese, and reserved bacon and cook over low heat just until the egg sets and the cheese melts. Add the pasta to warm it, and toss well. Transfer to a serving platter and serve immediately.

Makes 2 servings

Classic Egg Pasta

DEAN WHITEHEAD, ASSISTANT PRODUCTION COORDINATOR

3¾ cups flour
1 teaspoon salt
8 egg yolks
1 tablespoon olive oil plus extra
* for greasing*

Combine the flour and salt in a large, sturdy bowl, and make a well in the center. Set aside ½ cup of this mixture for dusting the countertop. In a small bowl, blend the egg yolks, ½ cup water, and 1 tablespoon olive oil. Pour the egg mixture into the well, incorporating the flour quickly with a sturdy spoon. When the dough forms a sticky ball, turn out onto a dusted countertop. (All the flour may not be incorporated at this point.) Knead the pasta for 5 to 10 minutes, working in any remaining flour. Add a little water slowly as needed, to form a smooth and elastic dough. Shape the dough into a ball, and lightly oil the surface with 1 teaspoon olive oil. Refrigerate for 1 hour in a covered bowl. Remove the dough from the refrigerator and cut it into 12 uniform pieces. Keep the remaining dough covered while you work with each piece. Gently knead and flatten the dough, adding a few drops of water if needed. Run the dough through a pasta machine until it reaches desired thickness. Dry on a drying rack. Pasta may be cooked immediately or frozen. Cooking time generally ranges from 30 seconds to 2 minutes.

Makes 8 servings (about 3 pounds)

Fettucine Al'Sausage

ANNE L. ANDERSON, PRODUCTION

*1 pound smoked sausage, cut into
¼-inch slices*
½ cup chopped mushrooms
4 cloves garlic, minced
5 tablespoons butter
1½ cups half-and-half
½ cup grated Parmesan cheese
¾ pound fettucine
¼ teaspoon black pepper

In a skillet, sauté the sausage, mushrooms, and half the garlic with the butter until the sausage is lightly browned. Add the half-and-half and bring to a boil, stirring constantly. Add ¼ cup of the Parmesan cheese, reduce heat, and simmer for 5 minutes, stirring constantly. Meanwhile, boil water and cook the fettucine until al dente. Drain and add the pasta to the skillet. Add the remaining ¼ cup Parmesan cheese, remaining garlic, and pepper. Toss well.

Makes 6 servings

Salmon and Asparagus Fettucine with Basil Sauce

CYNTHIA SCARBOURGH, MOTOR HOME OWNER

12 ounces skinless salmon fillet
1½ cups asparagus tips
½ cup plus 1 teaspoon butter
1 teaspoon chopped fresh basil
½ teaspoon chopped fresh oregano
2 tablespoons minced garlic
1½ teaspoons minced scallions
½ teaspoon plus a pinch of salt
⅓ cup whipping cream
1 cup grated Parmesan cheese
½ pound fettucine
¾ cup seeded, diced tomatoes
¼ cup Chardonnay wine

Remove any bones from the salmon and cut it into ½-inch pieces. Set aside. Bring a pot of salted water to a boil and blanch the asparagus tips for 1 minute, then rinse to cool and set aside. Prepare the basil sauce by melting ½ cup butter in a skillet. Add the basil, oregano, garlic, scallions, and ½ teaspoon salt. Cook over medium heat for 3 minutes. Then whisk in the cream and bring to a boil. Reduce the sauce for 10 minutes, stirring constantly. Lower the heat to a simmer and blend in the Parmesan cheese until smooth.

Cook the pasta in boiling salted water until al dente. Meanwhile, in a large pan over medium heat, melt 1 teaspoon butter with a pinch of salt. Add the salmon and cook until it begins to turn pale. Add the asparagus tips and tomatoes and cook for 2 minutes. Add the wine and simmer until the liquid is reduced by half. Then add the basil sauce to the pan of salmon and toss in the cooked pasta. Simmer for 1 to 2 minutes until everything is heated through. Serve with grated Parmesan cheese.

Makes 4 servings

Fusilli with Tuna Sauce

MARY WEAVER DODSON, ART DIRECTOR

2 tablespoons olive oil
4 anchovy fillets (optional)
3 cloves garlic, minced
1 can (28 ounces) crushed
  Italian tomatoes
¾ tablespoon light or dark
  brown sugar
1 can (6½ ounces) tuna in
  olive oil
Salt and black pepper to taste
1 pound fusilli or spaghetti
2 tablespoons chopped Italian
  parsley
2 teaspoons chopped capers

Heat the olive oil in a skillet. Add the anchovies, if using, and garlic. Sauté over medium heat until the garlic is tender. Stir in the tomatoes and brown sugar and bring to a boil. Reduce heat and simmer for 10 to 15 minutes. Stir in the tuna, including its oil. Simmer for 5 minutes longer. Season to taste with salt and pepper. In boiling water, cook the fusilli until al dente and drain. Place in a large, warmed serving bowl. Add the sauce and toss very gently to combine. Serve immediately sprinkled with parsley and capers to garnish.

Makes 4 servings

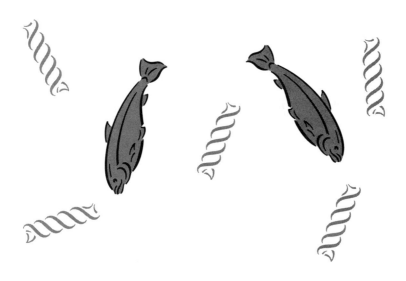

Quick Linguine and Clam Sauce

PETE JULIANO, LOCATION MANAGER

1 pound linguine
½ cup plus 1 tablespoon olive oil
4 cloves garlic, minced
1 can (6 ounces) chopped clams
½ cup dry white wine
1 teaspoon minced parsley
1 teaspoon dried sweet basil or 2
  leaves fresh sweet basil, minced
1 teaspoon dried oregano
¼ teaspoon sugar
Crushed red pepper to taste
½ teaspoon black pepper
Salt to taste
¼ teaspoon crushed anise seed
1 tablespoon grated Romano
  cheese

Cook the linguine according to package directions, adding 1 tablespoon olive oil. Drain and set aside. In a large skillet, heat ½ cup olive oil, add the garlic, and sauté, being careful not to burn the garlic. Add the clams and their juice, wine, parsley, basil, oregano, sugar, red pepper, black pepper, salt, and anise seed. Cook for 7 to 10 minutes, until the seasonings are blended. In a serving bowl, pour the clam sauce over the linguine and mix. Serve with grated Romano cheese.

Makes 4 servings

Linguine and White Clam Sauce

EILEEN BRENNAN, ACTRESS

5 cloves garlic, minced
¼ cup extra-virgin olive oil
1 can (21 ounces) minced
  clams, drained
½ cup clam broth

Sauté the garlic in the olive oil until golden. Add the minced clams, stirring for 3 minutes. Add the clam broth, wine, parsley, basil, oregano, and pepper. Cover and simmer for 5 minutes. In a separate pot, boil the fresh

½ cup dry white wine
½ cup chopped parsley
1 teaspoon dried basil
1 teaspoon dried oregano
1 teaspoon black pepper
1 dozen fresh clams, scrubbed
  (optional)
½ pound linguine
1 tablespoon grated Parmesan
  cheese

clams, if using, until they open. Discard any clams that feel extra heavy or do not open. Boil water and cook the linguine until al dente. Drain. Serve the sauce over the linguine and garnish with Parmesan cheese and fresh clams.

Makes 2 servings

Low-Fat Vegetable Pasta

LAINIE MILLER, SCRIPT SUPERVISOR

1½ cups chopped broccoli
1 large carrot, peeled and chopped
8 medium mushrooms, sliced
1 pound ramen noodles
1½ tablespoons salsa

*P*lace the broccoli and carrot in a pot, cover with water, and boil, covered. Turn down the heat and allow to cool for 10 minutes, covered. Add the mushrooms and cook for an additional 5 minutes. In a second small, covered pot, boil the noodles for 3 minutes. Drain any excess water from the noodles and stir in the salsa. Add the vegetables and blend. Serve immediately.

Makes 1 serving

Pasta DiCicco

BOBBY DICICCO, ACTOR

3 cloves garlic, minced
½ cup extra-virgin olive oil
8 ripe but firm Roma or plum
  tomatoes, cored and chopped
Salt and black pepper to taste
2 tablespoons chopped fresh
  basil leaves
1 teaspoon sugar (optional)
1 pound linguine or spaghetti

In a large skillet, lightly sauté the garlic in the olive oil. Add the tomatoes, season with salt and pepper, and cook for 10 minutes over medium heat, stirring occasionally. Add the basil and sugar, if desired. Reduce heat and simmer for 10 minutes. In a separate pot, prepare the linguine according to package directions. When ready, pour the sauce over the linguine and serve with crusty bread.

Makes 4 servings

Pasta Verde

MARY WEAVER DODSON, ART DIRECTOR

5 slices bacon
1 pound spaghetti or other pasta
⅓ teaspoon salt
1 package (10 ounces) frozen
  chopped spinach, cooked but
  not drained
2 cloves garlic, minced
⅛ teaspoon black pepper
½ cup creamy-style cottage cheese
⅓ cup grated Parmesan cheese

In a skillet, cook the bacon until crisp: drain, reserving 2 tablespoons drippings. Crumble the bacon and set aside. Boil the pasta in salted water for 10 to 12 minutes or until al dente. Set aside. Place the reserved bacon drippings, undrained spinach, garlic, and pepper in a blender or food processor and blend until smooth. Add the cottage cheese and blend until smooth. Pour the spinach mixture over the pasta and toss. Sprinkle individual servings with crumbled bacon and Parmesan cheese. Serve immediately.

Makes 8 servings

Pasta Puttanesca Sauce

DON PIKE, MEN'S WARDROBE SUPERVISOR

¼ cup olive oil
6 medium cloves garlic,
  coarsely chopped
4 medium yellow onions,
  finely chopped
1 can (28 ounces) whole tomatoes
1 tablespoon dried basil
1 teaspoon salt
1 teaspoon black pepper

In large skillet, heat the olive oil over medium heat. Add the garlic and onions and sauté for 5 to 7 minutes. Add the tomatoes, breaking them up with a fork. Stir in the basil, salt, and pepper. Reduce heat and simmer for 15 to 20 minutes. Serve over spaghetti, linguine, or fettucine. For variations, add real bacon bits, cooked, shredded chicken, or canned, flaked tuna during the last 5 minutes of cooking.

Makes 3 cups: enough for 6 servings

Fresh Pasta with Parmesan, Tomatoes, and Arugula

DEAN WHITEHEAD, ASSISTANT PRODUCTION COORDINATOR

6 Roma or plum tomatoes, seeded
  and coarsely chopped
3 bunches arugula, stems removed,
  coarsely chopped
⅓ cup extra-virgin olive oil
2 pounds Classic Egg Pasta (see
  Index) or pasta of your choice
½ cup grated Parmigiano-
  Reggiano cheese
Freshly ground black pepper to
  taste

Preheat the oven to 325°F. Place the tomatoes, arugula, and oil in a large serving bowl and toss. Place the bowl in the oven to heat for 10 minutes, together with serving bowls or plates. Cook the pasta in boiling water for 10 minutes or until al dente. Drain and return to the same pot. Remove the warmed tomatoes and arugula from the oven and add to the pasta. Mix in the cheese and toss. Season with pepper and serve immediately.

Makes 8 servings

THE *Murder, She Wrote* COOKBOOK

Pasta Turketti

GEORGE DYE, ASSISTANT CAMERA OPERATOR

1½ to 2 cups cooked, chopped
  chicken or turkey
¼ cup diced pimientos
¼ cup chopped green bell pepper
½ small yellow onion, chopped
1 can (10¾ ounces) cream of
  mushroom soup, undiluted
½ cup turkey broth or water
½ teaspoon salt
Ground black pepper to taste
½ pound sharp Cheddar cheese,
  shredded (1¾ cups)
¾ pound spaghetti, broken into 2-
  inch pieces, cooked, and drained

Preheat the oven to 350°F. In a 1½-quart casserole dish, combine the turkey, pimientos, green pepper, and onion. Pour in the soup and broth. Add salt and pepper, 1¼ cups of the cheese, and the spaghetti. Toss gently until the spaghetti is well coated. Sprinkle the remaining ½ cup of cheese on top. Bake for 45 minutes.

Makes 6 servings

Penne Matriciana

ROBB CURTIS-BROWN, ACTOR

8 thick slices bacon
4 tablespoons olive oil
1 large yellow onion, coarsely
  chopped
6 cloves garlic, minced
½ teaspoon dried thyme
½ cup dried marjoram
¾ cup chopped fresh basil

In a large skillet, cook the bacon in the olive oil. Drain on paper towels and set aside. Reserve 4 tablespoons of the oil in the pan. Sauté the onion, garlic, thyme, and marjoram in this oil until soft, making sure not to brown the onions or the garlic. Add the basil and chicken, if using. Cook the chicken until it is white and firm. Crumble reserved bacon

3 boneless chicken breasts, cut into
  strips (optional)
18 Roma or plum tomatoes, cored,
  seeded, and chopped
Salt and black pepper to taste
1 pound penne pasta
½ cup grated Parmesan or
  Romano cheese

and add to the pan along with the tomatoes. Cook over medium heat for 10 to 15 minutes. Season with salt and pepper to taste. Meanwhile, boil water for the pasta and cook until al dente. Drain and return the pasta to the pot. Add the sauce to the pasta and stir. Serve immediately garnished with Parmesan cheese.

Makes 8 servings

Tagliatelle al Checca

KELLY CANTLEY, SECOND ASSISTANT DIRECTOR

1 pound tagliatelle or fettucine
8 fresh Roma or plum tomatoes,
  cored and diced
¼ cup fresh chopped basil
⅛ teaspoon crushed red pepper
3 tablespoons olive oil
1 cup cubed mozzarella cheese

In boiling salted water, cook the pasta until al dente. Drain and set aside. While pasta is cooking sauté the tomatoes, basil, and red pepper in the olive oil until the tomatoes are soft but not mushy. Add to the cooked pasta and toss. Add the mozzarella and toss until the cheese just begins to melt. Serve with garlic bread and green salad.

Makes 4 to 6 servings

Tomato Basil Pasta Sauce

JEFF WHITE, ELECTRICIAN

2 tablespoons olive oil
2 cloves garlic, minced
¼ cup sliced scallions
¼ cup diced mushrooms
3 to 4 large tomatoes or 8 Roma
  or plum tomatoes, peeled, cored,
  and diced
2½ tablespoons chopped fresh basil
¼ teaspoon cayenne pepper
½ teaspoon Cajun seasoning
  (optional)
Ground black pepper to taste
½ cup grated Parmesan cheese
  (optional)

*I*n a large skillet, heat the oil. Add the garlic and scallions and sauté for 1 minute. Add the mushrooms and sauté for 1 more minute. Stir in the tomatoes, basil, cayenne pepper, Cajun seasoning, if using, and black pepper. Cook for 2 minutes, stirring frequently. Serve with pasta and grated Parmesan cheese. For variations, add cooked chicken, turkey, or Italian sausage when you add the tomatoes.

Makes 4 cups: enough for 4 to 6 servings

Veal with Artichokes and Linguine

LEE SMITH, DIRECTOR

Salt to taste
1 pound veal scaloppine, cut into
  ½-inch-wide strips
1 cup flour, or enough to coat veal
¼ cup olive oil

*S*alt the veal and coat lightly with flour. In a large skillet, heat the olive oil. Add the veal and brown on all sides, about 8 minutes. Add the lemon slices, basil, artichoke hearts, wine, and chicken broth. Simmer for 5 min-

½ lemon, seeded and thinly sliced
1 tablespoon chopped fresh basil or
   1 teaspoon dried basil
4 large artichoke hearts (fresh,
   frozen, or canned), cooked and
   thinly sliced
½ cup marsala wine
½ cup chicken broth
1 pound linguine, cooked and
   drained
Grated Parmesan cheese to taste

utes. Toss the veal mixture with the linguine. Serve at once garnished with grated Parmesan cheese.

Makes 4 servings

Vegetarian Lasagna

DEBORAH HUSS, MAKEUP

1 pound small-curd cottage cheese
1 pound mozzarella cheese, grated
2 large eggs
1 package (10 ounces) frozen
   chopped broccoli, thawed and
   completely drained
1 jar (32 ounces) spaghetti sauce
Dried oregano to taste
Salt and black pepper to taste
1 pound lasagna or wide noodles,
   uncooked

In a large bowl, mix together the cottage cheese, one-third of the mozzarella cheese, the eggs, broccoli, spaghetti sauce, oregano, salt, and pepper. Grease a 9 by 13-inch baking pan and cover the bottom with a thin layer of sauce. Add half the noodles, then half of the remaining sauce. Repeat layer with the noodles and remaining sauce mixture. Top with the remaining mozzarella cheese. Chill overnight. Preheat the oven to 350°F. Before baking, pour 1½ cups cold water around the edges of the pan, not in the center. Bake, lightly covered, for 1¼ hours, then let set for 15 minutes. For variations, add other vegetables, such as spinach or zucchini.

Makes 10 servings

Low-Fat High-Energy Pasta

CASEY BIGGS, ACTOR

¾ pound pasta, any type
6 to 8 fresh Roma or plum
  tomatoes, cored and diced
¾ cup red wine vinegar
Italian spices to taste (any
  combination of basil,
  oregano, and garlic)
1 heaping tablespoon of
  non-fat ricotta cheese
Tabasco sauce to taste
Salt and black pepper to taste

*I*n a large pot, boil water, add salt, and cook the pasta until al dente. Drain. In a large bowl, mix the tomatoes with the vinegar and spices. Add the pasta and mix in the cheese until melted. Season with Tabasco sauce, salt, and pepper to taste.

Makes 2 servings

Vodka Pasta

WILLIAM GALLO, ACTOR

1 pound rigatoni
3 chicken breasts, boned, skinned,
  and diced
2 to 3 tablespoons olive oil
Garlic salt to taste
1 pound fresh mushrooms, washed
  and sliced
4 tablespoons unsalted butter
½ cup vodka
1 pint whipping cream
1 cup spaghetti sauce
Pinch of parsley flakes

*C*ook the pasta according to package directions. Sauté the chicken in the olive oil and season lightly with garlic salt. Set aside. Sauté the mushrooms in the butter for 3 to 4 minutes. Drain off the excess butter. Add the vodka to the mushrooms and cook over medium heat until the vodka cooks off. Add the whipping cream to the mushroom mixture in the pan, reduce heat, and stir until it begins to thicken. Slowly stir in the spaghetti sauce until the mixture is pink, being careful not to add too much sauce. Add the parsley and basil.

Pinch of dried basil
½ cup grated Parmesan cheese

Add the chicken to this mixture and cook over medium heat until the chicken is warmed through. Pour the sauce over the pasta and sprinkle with Parmesan cheese. Serve with green salad and crusty Italian bread.

Makes 4 servings

Windom's Last Meal
(Caviar and Grits)

WILLIAM WINDOM, ACTOR

1 cup grits
1 cup wild rice
2 tablespoons unsalted butter,
* softened*
4 teaspoons beluga caviar

Cook the grits and wild rice according to package instructions. In a serving bowl toss together the cooked grits, wild rice, butter, and caviar. Serve warm with a bottle of chilled champagne.

Makes 2 servings

Curried Almond Rice

TEENA HEUSSER, WARDROBE

2 cloves garlic, minced
1 yellow onion, chopped
1½ cups basmati rice
1½ tablespoons butter or
  vegetable oil
3 cups chicken broth
3 tablespoons yellow curry powder
1 teaspoon salt
¾ cup toasted, unsalted slivered
  almonds

*S*auté the garlic, onion, and uncooked rice in the butter until the onion is translucent and the rice is browned. Add the chicken broth, curry powder, salt, and toasted almonds. Stir well. Cover and simmer for 20 to 25 minutes. This dish reheats in the microwave very nicely.

Makes 4 servings

Dirty Rice

TERI NOEL, ACTRESS

2 tablespoons vegetable oil
2 tablespoons flour
1 cup chopped yellow onion
1 cup chopped celery
½ cup chopped green bell pepper
2 cloves garlic, minced
½ pound ground beef
½ pound ground pork
½ pound chicken giblets, chopped
2 teaspoons salt
¾ teaspoon ground black pepper
¾ teaspoon crushed red pepper
1 cup chicken broth or water

*I*n a large skillet, heat the oil. Add the flour slowly and cook until the flour is deep red-brown. Stir constantly and be careful not to let the flour burn. Add the onion, celery, green pepper, and garlic and cook until tender. Stir in the beef, pork, giblets, salt, and

3 cups cooked rice
1 cup sliced scallions
½ cup raisins (optional)

peppers. Brown the meat, then add the broth. Cover and simmer for 25 minutes. Stir in the rice, scallions, and raisins, if using. Cook for 5 minutes. Serve with corn bread.

Makes 8 servings

Red-Eye Rice

JEFF WHITE, ELECTRICIAN

3 cups long-grain rice
3 cups shredded Cheddar cheese
3½ cups shredded Monterey
   Jack cheese
3½ cups medium or hot salsa
2½ cups frozen whole kernel
   corn, thawed
2 cups sour cream
1 jar (4 ounces) pimientos
1 can (4 ounces) diced green chilies
1 can (4 ounces) diced olives

*P*lace the rice and 4 cups water in a 4-quart Dutch oven and cover. Bring to a boil then reduce heat. Cook for 20 minutes. Do not lift the cover. Preheat the oven to 350°F. Remove from heat and let stand, covered, 10 minutes. In a medium bowl, mix together 2 cups of the Cheddar cheese, 2¼ cups of the Monterey Jack cheese, 2 cups of the salsa, 1¾ cups of the corn, all the sour cream, pimientos, chilies, and olives. Add the cooked rice. Turn the mixture into a 9 by 13 by 2-inch or a 4-quart baking dish. Top with the remaining cheese, salsa, and corn. Bake, uncovered, for 25 to 30 minutes, or until heated through. To prepare this as a main dish, add cooked chicken or turkey.

Makes 10 to 12 servings

Red Pepper Risotto

DENISE GENTILE, ACTRESS

1 large yellow onion, sliced
6 cloves garlic, minced
½ cup chopped fresh parsley
½-inch piece fresh ginger, peeled
    and shaved
6 tablespoons olive oil
6 tablespoons chopped, roasted
    red peppers
2 tablespoons butter
½ cup red wine
2 teaspoons mild curry paste
Pinch of salt
½ teaspoon lemon pepper
½ teaspoon black pepper
¼ teaspoon crushed red pepper
1 cup Arborio rice
4½ cups boiling water
½ cup grated Parmesan cheese
2 cups chopped, fresh mushrooms

Sauté the onion, garlic, parsley, and ginger in the olive oil until lightly browned. Add the roasted peppers, butter, wine, curry paste, salt, and peppers and stir well. Add the uncooked rice and lower the heat to a simmer. Then add 1 cup of the boiling water and stir constantly until absorbed. Continue stirring as you add the rest of the water, 1 cup at a time, waiting until each cup is absorbed before adding the next. Taste the dish as you go along to be sure that the rice is fully cooked near the end. Just before the last cup of water is completely absorbed, add the Parmesan cheese and the mushrooms and mix well. Continue cooking until all the water is absorbed and the rice is tender. Total cooking time is approximately ½ hour.

Makes 4 servings

Simple Risotto

ANDREA MARKS, FOODSTYLIST FROM BRUCE'S CATERING
(AS FEATURED IN THE EPISODE "PROOF IN THE PUDDING")

½ cup chopped white onion
2 cloves garlic, minced
¼ cup olive oil
2 cups Arborio rice

Sauté the onions and garlic in the oil until pearl-colored. Then add the uncooked rice and stir for 2 to 3 minutes. Add the white wine and stir until it's absorbed. In a separate

½ cup white wine
5⅓ cups stock, any type (chicken, vegetable, beef, or clam)
Parmesan cheese to taste

pot, boil the stock. Add the stock to the rice mixture, 1 cup at a time, until it's absorbed. Keep stirring or it will get lumpy. The risotto is done when all the stock is absorbed and the rice is tender, approximately 20 minutes. Serve immediately. Garnish with grated Parmesan cheese, if desired. To make this ahead of time, undercook and leave at room temperature until just before it's needed, then finish cooking and serve.

Makes 6 servings

Southwestern Macaroni and Cheese

VERA YURTCHUK, MAKEUP ARTIST

1 pound macaroni
2 teaspoons butter
2 large eggs, beaten
3 cups shredded Monterey Jack cheese
3 cups shredded sharp or extra-sharp Cheddar cheese
2 teaspoons dry mustard
1 teaspoon salt
2 cups milk

Preheat the oven to 350°F. Cook the macaroni in water until tender and drain thoroughly. Put the macaroni back in the pot and stir in the butter and eggs. Combine both cheeses together and add 4 cups of the cheeses to the macaroni, leaving 2 cups aside. Stir well. Pour the macaroni and cheese mixture into a large buttered casserole dish. In a separate bowl, mix the mustard and salt with 1 tablespoon hot water and add this to the milk. Then pour the mustard and milk mixture evenly over the macaroni. Sprinkle the remaining 2 cups of cheese on top. Bake for 45 to 60 minutes, or until the custard is set and the top is crusty.

Makes 8 servings

Tabouli

PHIL SHOFNER, PROP MAN

½ teaspoon salt
1 cup bulgur wheat
2 tablespoons olive oil
Black pepper to taste
2 cloves garlic, minced
2 tablespoons chopped fresh chives
2 teaspoons chopped fresh mint
  leaves
Juice of 1 or 2 lemons
⅓ cup chopped fresh parsley

*B*oil 2 cups water with the salt. Add the bulgur wheat and bring back to a boil. Remove from heat. Cover and let set for 15 minutes. Drain off excess water and chill for 4 hours. Toss thoroughly with all other ingredients.

Makes 4 servings

Wild Rice and Sausage Stuffing

RANDY MAYFIELD, CONSTRUCTION

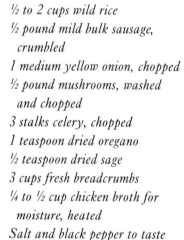

½ to 2 cups wild rice
½ pound mild bulk sausage,
  crumbled
1 medium yellow onion, chopped
½ pound mushrooms, washed
  and chopped
3 stalks celery, chopped
1 teaspoon dried oregano
½ teaspoon dried sage
3 cups fresh breadcrumbs
¼ to ½ cup chicken broth for
  moisture, heated
Salt and black pepper to taste

*C*ook the wild rice according to package directions. In a large skillet, brown the sausage until it begins to lose its pink color. Drain off excess fat. Add the onion, mushrooms, and celery and continue cooking until the vegetables are slightly softened and the sausage is fully cooked. Stir in 3 cups cooked wild rice, the oregano, sage, and breadcrumbs. Add warm chicken broth to moisten and season with salt and pepper to taste. Mix gently. This makes enough for a 10- to 14-pound turkey. To cook separately, place the stuffing in a buttered 3-quart casserole dish, cover, and bake at 350°F for 40 minutes.

Makes 8 cups

SEVEN

Vegetables

"I've played so many country women in my career that when I got the call to appear on an upcoming episode of Murder, She Wrote *as a farm wife, I just figured one more couldn't hurt. When I arrived on the set Angela Lansbury greeted me herself and said, 'Beth Grant, we are so happy to have you with us.' I was thrilled she even knew my name and to top it off she made me feel like a queen all week long. The cast and crew were great, too, and they made me feel right at home. We all had a good laugh when I walked onto the set kitchen, put on my obligatory apron, and asked, 'Now, who wants some corn bread?'"*

—*Beth Grant, actress*

Artichoke Pie

RON MASAK, ACTOR

½ cup chopped yellow onion

4 tablespoons butter or margarine

1 tablespoon flour

½ cup half-and-half

½ cup sour cream

4 large eggs, beaten

Salt and black pepper to taste

¼ teaspoon ground nutmeg

2 teaspoons minced parsley

2 packages (9 ounces each) frozen
  artichoke hearts, cooked

1 baked 9-inch piecrust

½ cup shredded Cheddar cheese

½ cup shredded Swiss cheese

¼ cup grated Parmesan cheese

Preheat the oven to 350°F. Sauté the onion in the butter or margarine until tender but not browned. Stir in the flour and blend well Add the half-and-half. Cook and stir until thickened. In a small bowl, combine the sour cream, eggs, salt, pepper, nutmeg, and parsley, then add to the sautéed onions. Place a layer of artichoke hearts in the bottom of the piecrust. Sprinkle the Cheddar cheese over the top. Add another layer of artichokes and top with Swiss cheese. Pour the egg and onion mixture over the layered artichokes and top with Parmesan cheese. Bake for 45 minutes.

Makes 4 servings

Chilled Asparagus and Vinaigrette

LEANN HUNLEY, ACTRESS

1 pound fresh asparagus

¼ cup fresh lemon juice

¾ cup olive oil

2 tablespoons Dijon mustard

2 medium tomatoes, cored and
  diced

In a large pot, steam the asparagus for 4 to 5 minutes, until tender. Remove from heat, drain, and chill. In a small bowl, whisk together the lemon juice, olive oil, and mustard until thoroughly mixed. Add the tomatoes, basil, and capers. Chill. Pour half the

⅓ cup fresh chopped basil
2 tablespoons capers

dressing over the asparagus and serve. The extra dressing is also great on salads or on any fresh steamed vegetable.

Makes 1½ cups

Cauliflower Fritters

LEON SINGER, ACTOR

1 cup dry white wine
3 medium heads cauliflower,
  leaves removed
1½ cups shredded Monterey
  Jack cheese
1 cup all-purpose flour
4 large eggs, lightly beaten
4 tablespoons vegetable oil
Salt to taste

*I*n a large pot, combine the wine and 2 cups water, and boil the whole cauliflowers until just tender (do not overcook). Cool the cauliflower and separate each head into 6 large pieces. Push a little cheese into the branches of each piece, pressing cauliflower and cheese together to make them adhere. Dip each piece into flour, coating all sides, then dip into the beaten eggs. The eggs should stick to the flour coating, but if they slide off give each piece a little more flour. Heat the vegetable oil in a large skillet and fry the fritters until golden. Season with salt and serve with Serrano Chili Sauce (see Index).

Makes 8 servings

Moroccan Curried Eggplant

ROBB CURTIS-BROWN, ACTOR

2 eggplants, cut into 1-inch cubes
1 tablespoon salt
¼ cup olive oil
½ large Spanish onion, chopped
4 cloves garlic, minced
1 tablespoon hot curry powder
½ teaspoon crushed red pepper
½ cup raisins
1 tablespoon balsamic vinegar

Place the eggplant in a large colander and sprinkle with salt. Weight the top of the eggplant with a plate and a heavy dish or pan. Let the eggplant drain at least ½ hour then rinse and pat dry with paper towels. Heat the olive oil and sauté the onion and garlic until soft. Do not brown. Add the eggplant, curry powder, and red pepper. Cook the eggplant, stirring, for about 20 to 25 minutes, until it is very soft. You may need to add a little extra oil. Be careful that it does not stick and burn. Add the raisins and vinegar and stir. Serve at any temperature.

Makes 10 servings as a side dish

Eggplant Parmesan

BRUCE KIRBY, ACTOR

1 large eggplant (1½ to 2 pounds)
3 eggs, lightly beaten
1½ cups dry breadcrumbs
¾ olive oil
1 jar (32 ounces) marinara or
  plain tomato sauce
¾ cup grated Parmesan cheese
¾ pound mozzarella cheese, sliced
2½ teaspoons dried oregano

Preheat the oven to 350°F. Cut the eggplant lengthwise into slices about ¼-inch thick. Dip the slices into the beaten eggs and then into the breadcrumbs. Sauté in the olive oil until both sides are golden brown, about 8 minutes. Line the bottom of a 2-quart casserole dish with ¼ cup of the tomato sauce. Top with half the eggplant, half the Parmesan cheese, mozzarella cheese, half the oregano, and half the remaining tomato sauce. Repeat to form another layer. Bake, uncovered, for 40 minutes.

Makes 6 servings

Microwave Green Bean Bake

CHRIS BATEMAN, ASSISTANT ELECTRICIAN

1 can (10¾ ounces) cream of mushroom soup, undiluted
½ cup milk
1 teaspoon soy sauce
Black pepper to taste
2 packages (9 ounces each) frozen French-style green beans, cooked and drained
2¾ ounces Durkee's French-fried onions

In a 2-quart microwave-safe casserole dish, combine the soup, milk, soy sauce, and black pepper and mix well. Stir in the green beans and half the onions. Cover and microwave on HIGH for 7 minutes. Halfway through cooking time, stir once and add the remaining onions on top.

Makes 6 servings

Green Beans with Honey Cashew Sauce

ZANNE SHAW, STAND-IN TO MS. LANSBURY

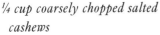

¼ cup coarsely chopped salted cashews
3 tablespoons unsalted butter or margarine
2 tablespoons honey
1 pound green beans, trimmed, cooked, and drained

Sauté the cashews in the butter over low heat for 5 minutes, until lightly browned. Add the honey and cook for 1 minute longer. Pour the cashew sauce over the beans, toss, and serve.

Makes 4 servings

Japanese Eggplant

STEVE UPTON, STUNTMAN

3 Japanese eggplants or small
  eggplants
2 tablespoons mild-tasting oil
¼ cup soy sauce
1½ tablespoons lemon juice
2 tablespoons dried tuna (optional)
1-inch piece fresh ginger, grated
  (about 1 ounce)
3 cups hot steamed rice

$\mathcal{S}$tarting about 1 inch from the top, cut the eggplants in half lengthwise and then, on the sides, make 2 additional lengthwise cuts, leaving the tops intact. In a skillet, heat the oil over medium-high heat. Add the eggplants, cover, and cook for about 5 minutes. Turn the eggplants over and add enough soy sauce to generously cover the bottom of the pan. Cover and cook for 10 to 15 minutes more, turning the eggplants if needed so they won't burn. Cook until soft and mushy. In a separate bowl for dipping, mix the remaining soy sauce and the lemon juice, a little at a time. The sauce should be a little sour but not too much. Sprinkle with dried tuna (found in Asian supermarkets), if using, and ginger. Serve with steamed rice.

Makes 3 servings

Stuffed Eggplant

MARY ALBEE, STUNT COORDINATOR

1 medium eggplant
1½ tablespoons margarine
¼ cup chopped yellow onion
2 cloves garlic, minced
6 mushrooms, coarsely chopped

$\mathcal{P}$reheat the oven to 350°F. Slice the eggplant in half lengthwise. Scoop out the pulp, leaving ¼ inch of shell. Chop the pulp and sauté in the margarine with the onion, garlic, and mushrooms until the onion is

½ cup cottage cheese
½ cup seasoned croutons
1¼ cups shredded mozzarella
  cheese
¼ teaspoon dried thyme
¼ cup parsley flakes
Salt and black pepper to taste
3 to 4 tablespoons salsa
2 tablespoons paprika

translucent and the eggplant is soft. Remove to a mixing bowl and combine with the cottage cheese, croutons, 1 cup of the mozzarella cheese, thyme, and parsley. Season with salt and black pepper and mix. Add the salsa. Fill the eggplant shells with the mixture and sprinkle with paprika. Bake in a greased pan, uncovered, for 25 minutes to ½ hour, or until the shells are soft and the filling is cooked. Remove from oven and sprinkle with the remaining mozzarella cheese and a little more paprika for color. Return to the oven and bake just until the cheese melts.

Makes 2 servings

Potatoes and Mushrooms Baked in Cream

HEIDI SVEDBERG, ACTRESS

2 pounds potatoes, peeled and
  sliced ¼ inch thick
½ pound chanterelle mushrooms
½ pound button mushrooms
2 cloves garlic, minced
2 tablespoons butter
Salt and black pepper to taste
1½ cups heavy cream

Preheat the oven to 375°F. Bring a large pot of salted water to a boil and parboil the potatoes for 2 minutes. Drain. Sauté the mushrooms and garlic in the butter with a pinch of salt, gently stirring for 5 minutes. Layer half the potatoes in a buttered casserole dish, then layer the mushrooms over them. Layer the remaining slices of potatoes on top. Season with salt and pepper. Pour the cream over the potatoes and bake for 45 minutes, or until almost all the cream is absorbed.

Makes 4 servings

Garlic Red Potatoes

MARK BURLEY, PRODUCER

6 tablespoons olive oil
6 cloves garlic, minced
12 to 15 small red potatoes,
 washed, dried, and quartered
4 basil leaves, washed, dried,
 and chopped

*P*reheat the oven to 375°F. Heat the olive oil in a roasting or baking pan. When the oil is hot, add the garlic. Stir in the potatoes and basil. Stir to coat the potatoes with oil and bake, uncovered, for 45 minutes to 1 hour on the top rack. Stir after ½ hour. When the potatoes are crisp on the outside but still moist on the inside, they are done. Drain on paper towels and serve hot.

Makes 4 servings

Mexican Potato-Cheese Fritters

LEON SINGER, ACTOR

6 large potatoes
1 cup grated Monterey Jack cheese
2 large eggs
½ teaspoon garlic powder or
 1 clove garlic, minced
½ teaspoon salt
¼ cup all-purpose flour
2 tablespoons vegetable oil
1½ cups sour cream
½ cup guacamole
1 cup salsa, homemade
 or from a jar

*C*ook the potatoes in a pot of boiling water until tender, about 15 minutes. Drain and lightly mash them. Mix the mashed potatoes with the cheese, eggs, garlic, and salt. Add a small amount of flour to the mixture to make the potatoes stick together. The amount of flour needed will depend on the size and type

of potatoes used. Form the potato mixture into 10 thick patties. Heat a large skillet and pour in a small amount of oil. Fry the patties, 2 or 3 at a time, until golden brown on each side. Serve the fritters with the sour cream and guacamole along with salsa on the side.

Makes 8 servings

Twice-Baked Potatoes

MIKE APPERSON, SECOND COMPANY GRIP

6 medium Idaho or russet
 baking potatoes
2 cups shredded Cheddar cheese
4 scallions, sliced
2 cups diced ham (optional)
1 pint sour cream
Salt and black pepper to taste

Precook the potatoes until half done in the microwave or oven. A fork should pierce the potatoes easily but the skins should stay firm. Cut in half lengthwise and scoop out the pulp, leaving the skins intact. Mix the potato pulp, 1½ cups of the cheese, scallions, ham, if using, and sour cream. Season with salt and black pepper to taste. Preheat the oven to 300°F. Stuff the skins with the mixture, sprinkle with the remaining cheese. Arrange the stuffed potatoes in a roasting pan or oven-proof dish and bake for ½ hour.

Makes 6 servings

Colcannon (Irish Mashed Potatoes)

BERNADETTE O'BRIEN, WARDROBE

1 pound kale, stems removed and
 leaves chopped
2½ teaspoons salt
4 pounds russet or Yukon gold
 potatoes, peeled and cut into
 1-inch cubes (about 10 cups)
1½ cups milk
¼ pound unsalted butter, softened
Freshly ground black pepper to
 taste

Wash the kale under cold water, drain, and place in a pan with ¼ cup water and ½ teaspoon salt. Cover tightly. Braise for 15 minutes, checking occasionally that the kale does not burn. Chop the kale finely or process in the food processor. In a large saucepan, cover the potatoes with cold salted water. Bring to a boil, partially covered, and cook for ½ hour or until tender. Drain the potatoes and mash them in the cooking pot. Turn the heat on low and fold the kale into the mashed potatoes. Gradually whisk in the milk and butter. Season with the remaining 2 teaspoons salt and freshly ground pepper. Serve immediately.

Makes 8 servings

Scalloped Potatoes with Cheese

RONNE TROUP, ACTRESS

1 clove garlic, cut in half
6 medium red potatoes, peeled and
 cut into ⅛-inch slices
2 tablespoons butter, melted
Salt and black pepper to taste
½ cup shredded Cheddar cheese
1 cup low-fat milk

Preheat the oven to 425°F. Rub a 10 by 6 by 2-inch baking dish with the cut side of the garlic and a little butter. Arrange half the potatoes in the dish and drizzle with half the melted butter. Sprinkle with salt and pepper. Top with half of the cheese. Repeat, using the rest of the potatoes, butter, and cheese.

Heat the milk in a saucepan and pour over the potatoes. Bake, uncovered, for 40 minutes, until crusty and creamy.

Makes 6 servings

Oregano Potatoes

RAMY ZADA, ACTOR

5 large baking potatoes, washed, peeled, and quartered
Juice of 1 lemon
3 tablespoons plus 2 teaspoons olive oil
2 tablespoons dried oregano
Salt and black pepper to taste

Preheat the oven to 450°F. Place the potatoes, lemon juice, 3 tablespoons olive oil, and oregano in a large, ovenproof pan and toss together. Bake for 1 hour. Stir the potatoes at least twice while baking to cook evenly. Season with salt and black pepper to taste. Drizzle with the remaining olive oil before serving.

Makes 4 servings

Oven-Roasted Herbed Potatoes

BILL LAYTON, CAMERA OPERATOR

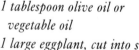

1 pound white rose potatoes, cut
 into 1½-inch cubes
1 pound red potatoes, cut into 1½-
 inch cubes
¼ cup extra-virgin olive oil
1 tablespoon dried rosemary
2 medium yellow onions, chopped
3 cloves garlic, minced
½ teaspoon curry powder
Salt and black pepper to taste
Paprika to taste

Preheat the oven to 375°F. Mix together the potatoes, olive oil, rosemary, onions, garlic, and curry powder in a large bowl. Turn into a large ovenproof dish. Add salt, black pepper, and paprika to taste and bake for 1¼ hours.

Makes 8 servings

Ratatouille

LORETTA SWIT, ACTRESS

1 tablespoon olive oil or
 vegetable oil
1 large eggplant, cut into small
 cubes
2 large yellow onions, chopped
4 large zucchini, sliced
2 large tomatoes, peeled, cored,
 and chopped
2 cloves garlic, minced
Salt and black pepper to taste

In a large soup kettle, heat the oil and add the eggplant. Cook for 7 to 10 minutes over medium heat. Add the onions and zucchini. Cook for another 15 minutes. Add the tomatoes, mixing them in well, because this is where the juices will come from. Add the garlic. Cook for 5 minutes more. Reduce heat, cover, and simmer for 45 minutes to 1 hour. The vegetables should be cooked through and the flavors well blended. Season with salt and pepper. This Provençal dish may be served hot or cold, as a side dish, as a kind of thick soup, or as a spread.

Makes 6 to 8 servings

Red Peppers in Oil

PAMELA PEITZMAN, MAKEUP

5 large red bell peppers
¼ cup olive oil
5 cloves garlic, minced
Salt to taste
Cayenne pepper to taste
3 tablespoons fresh lime juice
2 tablespoons fresh lemon juice

*B*roil the peppers until the skins turn black and begin to blister. Place the peppers in a sealed plastic bag for a few minutes to steam the skins loose. Peel the charred skin, remove the seeds, and cut into strips ½-inch wide. In a saucepan, cook the olive oil, garlic, salt, and cayenne pepper over low heat. Add the red peppers, lime juice, and lemon juice. Cook for about ½ hour. Serve at room temperature with thin slices of hard provolone cheese and Italian bread.

Makes 6 servings

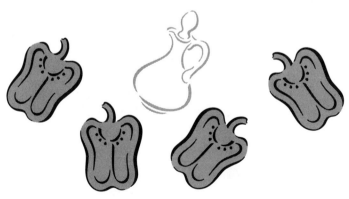

Baked Spinach and Rice

STEVE PERINI, DRIVER AND PROPS

1 large yellow onion, chopped
2 tablespoons vegetable oil
1 package (10 ounces) chopped spinach, cooked and drained
2 cups Minute Rice, cooked
¼ cup grated Romano cheese
¼ cup grated Parmesan cheese
1 pound ricotta cheese
4 large eggs, beaten
¼ cup Italian breadcrumbs

Preheat the oven to 350°F. Sauté the onion in the oil until translucent. Mix together the cooked spinach and rice in a large bowl. Add the cheeses, 3 of the eggs and the onions, and mix well. Pour into a greased 7 by 11 by 2-inch baking pan. Pour the remaining egg over the top and the breadcrumbs. Bake for 20 minutes. Then increase the oven temperature to 400°F and bake for 20 minutes more, or until the top is nicely browned.

Makes 8 servings

Warm New Red Potatoes with Rosemary

MARK BURLEY, PRODUCER

2 pounds small new red potatoes (about 30)
2 tablespoons olive oil
1 teaspoon salt
2 tablespoons minced fresh rosemary leaves

In a large pot of boiling water, cook the potatoes for 12 to 15 minutes, until just done in the center when pierced with a fork. Drain and let cool slightly. While still warm, slice the potatoes in half and place in a large bowl. Toss with the olive oil, salt, and rosemary.

Makes 6 to 8 servings

Spanakopitta (Spinach Pie)

TALI FOREST-SMITH, ESTIMATOR

10 leeks, sliced and washed well
10 cloves garlic, minced
¼ cup olive oil
1 bunch Swiss chard, chopped
10 bunches fresh spinach, chopped
1 pound Greek or Bulgarian feta
  cheese, crumbled
2 cups cooked white rice
1 pound phyllo
1 pound butter, melted

Preheat the oven to 350°F. Sauté the leeks and garlic in the olive oil until soft. Add the Swiss chard and spinach and cook down. Stir in the feta cheese and cooked rice and set aside. Layer half the phyllo sheets in a large glass baking dish, brushing each sheet with melted butter. Keep the unused phyllo wrapped in a towel to prevent drying. Spread the spinach mixture evenly over the phyllo. Layer the remaining phyllo over the top, brushing each sheet with butter, especially the top sheet. Bake for 45 minutes, or until golden.

Makes 6 servings

Spinach Pie

FRANCE NUYEN, ACTRESS

1 bunch fresh spinach, washed thoroughly
4 tablespoons salted butter, melted
2 cups shredded sharp Cheddar cheese, at room temperature
½ cup flour
¼ teaspoon dry mustard
1 medium yellow onion, diced
1 pound mushrooms, sliced
4 tablespoons butter
⅔ cup milk
⅔ cup whipping cream
1 teaspoon ground nutmeg
Salt and black pepper to taste
6 large eggs

In a pot of boiling water, blanch the spinach. Drain well and set aside. In a medium bowl, combine the melted butter, cheese, flour, and dry mustard. Stir until well blended. Press this cheese crust into a 10 by 12-inch deep-dish fluted mold and set aside. Preheat the oven to 400°F. Sauté the onion and mushrooms in the butter until golden. Layer the spinach evenly in the cheese crust. Layer the onion and mushroom mixture on top of the spinach. In a small bowl, mix together the milk, cream, nutmeg, salt, pepper and eggs thoroughly and pour over the sautéed mixture. Cradle the mold with aluminum foil to avoid dripping. Bake for 20 minutes. Reduce the heat to 325°F and bake another ½ hour, or until an inserted knife comes out clean.

Makes 6 servings

Baked Butternut Squash

RAMY ZADA, ACTOR

1 large butternut squash
4 tablespoons butter
4 tablespoons Grand Marnier

*P*reheat the oven to 350°F. Cut the squash in half lengthwise and scoop out the seeds. With a fork, pierce the pulp of the squash, making sure the whole area is pierced. Slice the butter into pats and place 3 to 4 pats in each squash half. Pour the Grand Marnier over the squash. Bake for 45 minutes to 1 hour, or until a fork pierces the squash easily.

Makes 2 servings

Butternut Squash Mashed Potatoes

CURTIS BLANCK, ACTOR

1 small butternut squash
2 potatoes, peeled and diced
¼ cup butter

*P*reheat the oven to 400°F. Cut the squash in half and scoop out the seeds. Place the squash halves cut-side down on a lightly greased pan and bake for 1 hour. Scoop the pulp from the shells and set aside. Boil the potatoes, covered, for 15 minutes. Drain and mix the butter into the potatoes. Gradually add as much squash as desired. If the potatoes seem stiff, add a little chicken broth or milk until they reach the desired consistency.

Makes 6 servings

Vegetable Fritatta

TALI FOREST-SMITH, ESTIMATOR

5 white rose potatoes, peeled and thinly sliced
1 large yellow onion, thinly sliced
2 tablespoons olive oil
5 zucchini, thinly sliced
1 pound fresh mushrooms, thinly sliced
½ pound broccoli, chopped
1 dozen large eggs
¼ cup milk
Salt and black pepper to taste

Preheat the oven to 450°F. Place the potatoes and onion in a large, deep, ovenproof dish. Sprinkle with the olive oil. Bake for 15 minutes. Add the zucchini, mushrooms, and broccoli and bake for another 5 minutes. Whisk the eggs and milk with salt and pepper and pour over the vegetables. Reduce the heat to 350°F. Bake for 20 minutes, or until eggs are cooked. Serve warm or cold.

Makes 8 servings

Yapraks (Grape Leaves Stuffed with Meat and Rice)

DEBORAH HUSS, MAKEUP

1 pound lean ground beef or lamb

1 jar or can (1 pound) grape leaves

¼ cup rice, washed and drained

¼ cup plus 2 tablespoons tomato sauce or ¼ cup chopped fresh tomato and 2 tablespoons tomato sauce

Salt to taste

Allspice to taste

⅓ cup chopped fresh parsley

2 tablespoons vegetable oil

¼ cup toasted pine nuts (optional)

2 cups water

Juice of 1 large or 2 small lemons

In a large skillet, brown the beef. Rinse each grape leaf, remove the tough stems, and drape around the edge of a colander to drain. Gently mix together the beef, rice, ¼ cup tomato sauce, salt, allspice, parsley, 1 tablespoon of the oil, and the nuts, if using. Be careful not to overmix, as too much handling will make the mixture tough. Spread out each grape leaf, bottom side up. Fill with about 1 tablespoon of filling and roll loosely, tucking in the sides. Place the rolls in a large saucepan that has been lined with extra grape leaves. Arrange the rolls closely to prevent them from falling apart. In a mixing bowl, whisk together the water, remaining 2 tablespoons tomato sauce, and remaining 1 tablespoon oil. Pour over the grape leaf rolls to cover one-quarter of the depth of the pan. Cover and cook over low heat for 1 hour. A rolling boil will cause the yapraks to come apart. If pan is deep, place a heatproof plate over the yapraks to keep them in place. Check periodically to make sure there is sufficient sauce. Add more sauce if necessary, but be careful as too much will make the yapraks soggy. After cooking slowly for 1 hour, preheat the oven to 350°F, add the lemon juice, and transfer carefully to an ovenproof dish. Bake, uncovered, for ½ hour.

Makes 6 servings

163

Baked Zucchini

JAY CAPLAN, COSTUMER

4 cups grated unpeeled zucchini
2 cups instant biscuit mix
1 large yellow onion, diced
 (about 1 cup)
6 to 8 cloves garlic, minced
4 tablespoons fresh minced parsley
½ teaspoon dried oregano
5 large eggs, beaten
¾ cup grated Parmesan cheese
¾ cup shredded Monterey Jack
 cheese
¾ cup shredded Cheddar cheese
¾ cup vegetable oil
½ teaspoon salt

*P*reheat the oven to 350°F. Mix all the ingredients together in a large bowl and pour into a 9 by 13-inch greased pan. Bake for ½ hour to 35 minutes, or until golden brown. Cut into large pieces to serve as a side dish or small pieces to serve as appetizers.

Makes 4 servings

Stuffed Zucchini

DAVE MARSIK, SET LIGHTING

4 cups brown rice
1 lobster tail, cut into ½-inch
 cubes
½ pound shrimp, peeled and
 deveined
½ pound crabmeat, cut into ½-
 inch cubes
½ large white onion, chopped
4 cloves garlic, minced

*C*ook the brown rice according to package directions until about three-quarters done, about ½ hour. Set aside. Sauté the lobster, shrimp, crab, onion, and garlic in the butter for about 3 minutes. Set aside and allow to cool slightly. Preheat the oven to 350°F. Cut the zucchini in half lengthwise. Hollow out the centers with a melon baller or knife and spoon. They should resemble little canoes. In

2 tablespoons butter
2 large or 4 small zucchini
2 cups grated Parmesan cheese
1 cup white wine

a bowl, mix together the rice, sautéed seafood, 1 cup of the grated cheese, and stuff into the zucchini hollows. Arrange the zucchini in an ovenproof dish, baste with the wine, and cover tightly with aluminum foil. Bake for 45 minutes, or until tender. Open the foil, sprinkle the remaining 1 cup cheese on top, and place under the broiler, uncovered, for 1 minute or until the cheese melts.

Makes 4 servings

Zucchini with Bacon

TEENA HEUSSER, WARDROBE

3 strips bacon
1 medium red onion, chopped
3 medium zucchini, scored with fork and sliced ¼-inch thick

Fry the bacon until crispy and drain, reserving 2 tablespoons drippings. Sauté the onion in the reserved bacon drippings until translucent. Add the zucchini and sauté for 2 minutes. Add 2 tablespoons water, cover, and cook for 1 minute for firm zucchini or 2 minutes for softer zucchini. Remove from heat, add the crumbled bacon, and serve immediately.

Makes 2 to 3 servings

Scalloped Corn and Tomatoes

JAY CAPLAN, COSTUMER

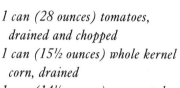

1 can (28 ounces) tomatoes, drained and chopped

1 can (15½ ounces) whole kernel corn, drained

1 can (14½ ounces) cream-style corn

2 large eggs, lightly beaten

¼ cup all-purpose flour

2 teaspoons sugar

½ to 1 teaspoon black pepper

6 tablespoons margarine or butter

1 medium yellow onion, finely chopped

½ teaspoon garlic powder

4 cups soft breadcrumbs

½ cup grated Parmesan cheese

*P*reheat the oven to 350°F. In a 2-quart casserole dish, mix together the tomatoes, kernel corn, cream-style corn, eggs, flour, sugar, and pepper. In a small saucepan, melt the margarine and cook the onion and garlic powder until the onion is tender but not browned. Remove from heat and stir in the breadcrumbs and Parmesan cheese. Sprinkle over the corn mixture and bake, uncovered, for 1 hour or until the top is browned and the inside is set.

Makes 12 servings

EIGHT

Sauces

"After spending so many years working indoors on sets, it was great to have a chance to shoot outdoors on location. In the episode I guest-starred on, I played the groundskeeper of a fabulous estate. We filmed it on the Disney ranch, a two-hundred-acre lot where many of the old Disney films were made. I had a dog that followed me around and I knew all the family's secrets. Those highbrow connections didn't help me any, though, when it came time for lunch. It was catered outside and I had to wait in line with everyone else. Is nothing fair?"

—Leon Singer, actor

Basil Pesto

JAMES ACHESON, ACTOR

6 large fresh basil leaves,
 finely chopped
2 cloves garlic
¾ cup freshly grated Romano or
 Parmesan cheese
⅓ cup walnuts or pine nuts
½ cup olive oil

In a food processor or blender, mix together the basil, garlic, cheese, and nuts. Add the oil slowly. The mixture should be the consistency of thick tomato sauce. Mix directly into hot pasta or add a dollop to flavor any tomato sauce.

Makes 1½ cups

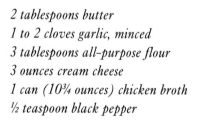

Garlic Cream Sauce

JOHN MALDONADO, MAKEUP

2 tablespoons butter
1 to 2 cloves garlic, minced
3 tablespoons all-purpose flour
3 ounces cream cheese
1 can (10¾ ounces) chicken broth
½ teaspoon black pepper

In a medium saucepan, melt the butter over medium heat until it sizzles. Add the garlic and cook for 1 minute, or until the garlic changes color, stirring occasionally. Add the flour, stirring until smooth. Add the cream cheese, broth, and pepper. Cook, stirring frequently, for 5 to 7 minutes, until mixture thickens. This is great over pork, lamb, beef, or steamed vegetables.

Makes 1½ cups

Simple Barbecue Sauce

SKIP MCNALLY, HAIRSTYLIST

¼ cup Worcestershire sauce
¼ cup cider or white vinegar
¼ cup water
¼ cup dark brown sugar
¼ cup ketchup

*C*ombine all the ingredients in a small saucepan and stir until well mixed. Simmer over medium–low heat for about 10 minutes.

Makes 1¼ cups

Hollandaise Sauce

TOM CULVER, WARDROBE

3 egg yolks
1 tablespoon fresh lemon juice
¼ pound (1 stick) butter, melted
2 tablespoons hot water
Cayenne pepper to taste
Salt to taste

*I*n the top of a double boiler over hot water, beat the egg yolks with a wire whisk until smooth. Add the lemon juice and gradually whisk in the melted butter, pouring in a thin stream. Slowly stir in the water, cayenne pepper, and salt. Continue to mix for 1 minute, until the sauce thickens. Serve immediately or keep over warm water for 1 to 2 hours, but don't try to keep it out too long without refrigerating. To correct a curdled hollandaise, whisk in 1 or 2 teaspoons of boiling water, one drop at a time. If that doesn't work, put an egg yolk in a bowl and add the curdled sauce very slowly, beating with a whisk.

Makes 1 cup

Shish Kabob Marinade

BUFFY SNYDER, WARDROBE SUPERVISOR

1½ cups mild-tasting oil
¾ cup soy sauce
¼ cup Worcestershire sauce
2 tablespoons dry mustard
2¼ teaspoons salt
⅓ cup fresh lemon juice
1 tablespoon black pepper
½ cup white wine vinegar
1½ teaspoons chopped parsley
2 cloves garlic, minced

Mix all ingredients and use to marinate shish kabobs.

Makes 2½ cups

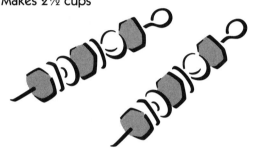

Spaghetti Meatball Sauce

PHIL BEESON, UTILITY SOUND TECHNICIAN

2 pounds lean ground beef
or ground turkey
2 large eggs
¼ cup white wine
4 yellow onions, finely chopped
5 cloves garlic, minced
½ cup plus 1 teaspoon chopped
parsley
¼ cup grated Parmesan cheese
3½ tablespoons olive or canola oil
2 cans (28 ounces each) whole
tomatoes
4 cans (8 ounces each) tomato
sauce

To make the meatballs: Mix together the ground beef or turkey, eggs, wine, 2 onions, 4 cloves garlic, 1 teaspoon parsley, and Parmesan thoroughly. Form into spoon-sized meatballs and brown in 1½ tablespoons oil. Remove from heat and set aside.

To make the sauce: Sauté the remaining 2 onions, 1 clove garlic, and ½ cup parsley in the remaining 2 tablespoons oil. When done, transfer to a large pot. Add the tomatoes, tomato sauce, tomato paste, mushrooms, oregano, and rosemary, and season with salt

170

2 cans (6 ounces each)
  tomato paste
½ pound fresh mushrooms, sliced
2 teaspoons dried oregano
1 teaspoon dried rosemary,
  crushed
Salt and black pepper to taste

and pepper. Add the meatballs and simmer for 2 hours, stirring often. As a variation, try adding 6 links hot, spicy sausages cut into ½-inch pieces when you add the meatballs.

Makes 8 cups

Simple Tomato Pasta Sauce

SUZANNE WAITE, SCRIPT SUPERVISOR

2 tablespoons olive oil
6 cloves garlic, minced
1 can (28 ounces) chopped
  tomatoes
8 fresh basil leaves
¼ pound fresh mushrooms, sliced
  (optional)

Heat the olive oil in a skillet and sauté the garlic for 1 minute. Add the tomatoes, basil, and mushrooms, if using. Sauté for 3 minutes. Pour over pasta. A pinch of sugar will make this sauce less acidic.

Makes 4 cups

Turkey Sausage Pasta Sauce

TEENA HEUSSER, WARDROBE

2 yellow onions, finely chopped

4 cloves garlic, minced

1 red bell pepper, chopped

1 yellow bell pepper, chopped

1 tablespoon olive oil

14 links Italian turkey
 sausage, browned and cut
 into 1-inch lengths

1 can (28 ounces) peeled,
 crushed Italian tomatoes

2 cans (6 ounces each)
 tomato paste

1 can (6½ ounces) sliced
 black olives

2 tablespoons chopped fresh
 sweet basil

1 tablespoon fresh tarragon

1 bay leaf

½ teaspoon ground black pepper

2 tablespoons chopped fresh
 oregano

2 teaspoons salt

2 teaspoons sugar

¼ pound mushrooms, sliced

Sauté the onions, garlic, red pepper, and yellow pepper in the olive oil until the onions are translucent. Transfer to a large cooking pot. Add the turkey sausage, tomatoes, tomato paste, olives, basil, tarragon, bay leaf, black pepper, oregano, salt, sugar, and 2 cups water. Simmer over low heat for 2 hours. Add the mushrooms and simmer at least 4 more hours. This is best made in advance and served the next day. Remove the bay leaf before serving.

Makes 6 cups

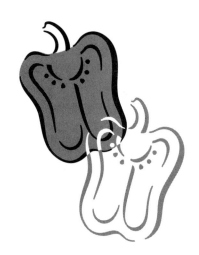

Serrano Chili Sauce

LEON SINGER, ACTOR

¼ cup vegetable oil
½ yellow onion, chopped
4 cloves garlic
2 serrano chilies, quartered
3 large tomatoes, quartered
1 large sprig cilantro, finely
  chopped

*H*eat the oil in a saucepan. Put the onion, garlic, chilies, tomatoes, and cilantro into a blender or food processor and chop finely. Add to the oil and cook over medium heat; foam will form at the beginning and will gradually disappear. When the foam subsides, the sauce is ready. The longer the sauce cooks, the thicker it will be.

Makes 3 cups

NINE

Breads and Sandwiches

"In the episodes I guest-starred on I always played the detective with a trench coat. Murder, She Wrote *was a great fantasy job. I got to play that part so often that I told the wardrobe people to hold my trench coat; I'll be back soon."*

—*Efrain Figueroa, actor*

Buttermilk Bread

ROBIN BEAUCHESNE, MAKEUP

2 packages (2 scant tablespoons)
 yeast
1¼ cups buttermilk
4½ cups flour
¼ cup vegetable shortening
2 tablespoons sugar
2 tablespoons baking powder
2 tablespoons salt
½ tablespoon butter, melted

Dissolve the yeast in ¾ cup warm water. Add the buttermilk, 2½ cups of the flour, shortening, sugar, baking powder, and salt. Blend well, scraping the bowl constantly. Beat with an electric mixer for 2 minutes at medium speed, scraping the bowl occasionally. Stir in the remaining flour. The dough should be slightly sticky. Turn the dough out on a well-floured board. Knead for 200 turns, about 10 minutes. Place the dough in a greased loaf pan and let rise in a warm place until it has doubled in size, about 1 hour. Preheat the oven to 425°F. Bake until golden brown. Brush the finished loaf with melted butter. As a variation, add 1 teaspoon onion powder to the yeast-and-water mixture.

Makes 1 loaf

Banana Bread

HUB BRADEN, PRODUCTION DESIGNER

2 large eggs
1½ cups sugar
5 ripe bananas
4 tablespoons butter, melted
1 teaspoon baking soda

Preheat the oven to 350°F. Mix the eggs, sugar, and ripe bananas (the riper the better) thoroughly with an electric mixer. Add the melted butter and mix. Add the baking soda, salt if using, baking powder, nutmeg,

1 teaspoon salt (optional)
3 teaspoons baking powder
1 tablespoon ground nutmeg
1 tablespoon ground cinnamon
1 tablespoon vanilla extract
5 cups flour
⅓ to ½ cup milk
11 ounces butterscotch chips,
 crushed
1½ cups pecans or walnuts,
 chopped

cinnamon, vanilla, flour and milk, and mix.
Do not let batter get too stiff while mixing.
After all the ingredients are mixed together,
fold in the butterscotch chips and nuts. Pour
into 2 greased loaf pans. Dust with flour. Bake
for 1 hour. Allow to cool for ½ hour on a wire
rack before serving.

Makes 2 loaves

Country Corn Bread Muffins

BETH GRANT, ACTRESS

2 cups cornmeal
½ teaspoon salt
½ teaspoon baking soda
2 teaspoons baking powder
2 large eggs
2 tablespoons vegetable oil
2 cups buttermilk

*P*reheat the oven to 400°F. In a large
 bowl, mix together all the ingredients.
Pour into a well-oiled, large muffin tin. Bake
for 25 minutes, until brown and crispy outside
and done inside. Serve hot with butter.
Alternatively, the corn bread batter can be
cooked by dropping spoonfuls onto a hot,
oiled skillet, or into a deep fryer.

Makes 12 muffins

Irish Boxties

BERNADETTE O'BRIEN, WARDROBE

¾ cup grated raw Yukon gold or Superior potatoes
1 cup mashed potatoes
1 cup all-purpose flour
3 tablespoons bacon fat or vegetable oil
1½ teaspoons salt
Freshly ground pepper to taste
2 tablespoons butter

Push the grated potatoes through a strainer with the back of a spoon. Reserve the potato water. Combine the grated potatoes and the mashed potatoes with a fork. Gradually beat in the flour 1 tablespoon at a time. Beat in 2 tablespoons of the bacon fat, and season with salt and pepper. Knead until smooth. If the dough gets too dry, add some reserved potato water. Cut the dough into 4 pieces. Flour a pastry surface and shape each piece into a pancake 5 inches in diameter. Cut an X on the top. Heat the remaining 1 tablespoon bacon fat in a large nonstick skillet. Add the boxties and cook for 15 minutes on each side or until golden brown. Slice the boxties into wedges, spreading butter over each wedge. Serve immediately. The butter melting into the boxtie is a real treat. For a breakfast, fry leftover boxties and serve with jam or maple syrup.

Makes 4 servings

Irish Soda Bread

TOM MASON, ACTOR

4 cups all-purpose flour
1½ teaspoons baking soda
2½ teaspoons baking powder
1 cup sugar
¼ teaspoon salt
3 tablespoons butter, softened
1½ cups raisins
2 tablespoons caraway seeds
1 cup buttermilk, at room
  temperature
2 large eggs, lightly beaten
Cinnamon and sugar to
  sprinkle on top

All ingredients should be at room temperature before making this recipe. Preheat the oven to 350°F. Mix together the flour, baking soda, baking powder, sugar, and salt. Cut in the butter and mix. The mixture should be crumbly. Add the raisins and caraway seeds. Add the buttermilk, a little at a time. Add the eggs. Mix all ingredients together until dough is formed. Transfer the dough to a floured surface and knead for about 5 minutes. Shape the dough into large ball. Cut the ball in half and form 2 balls. Cut a deep cross on top of each ball but do not flatten. Sprinkle the tops with cinnamon and sugar and place on a baking sheet. Bake for 1 hour. The dough will flatten a little as it bakes. Cool before cutting. The finished bread will have a cakey texture.

Makes 2 loaves

Mexican Corn Bread

JOANIE FRASCO, STAND-IN

1½ cups cottage cheese
1 cup yellow cornmeal
1 tablespoon butter, melted
1 can (14¾ ounces) creamed corn
2 teaspoons baking powder
¾ cup sugar
3 large eggs
¼ cup pimientos
1 can (7 ounces) green chilies
1 cup grated Cheddar cheese

Preheat the oven to 325°F. In a large bowl, combine all the ingredients. Mix well. The batter will be a little lumpy. Pour into a 9 by 12-inch greased baking dish and bake for 40 minutes. Cut into squares and serve warm or cold.

Makes 6 to 8 servings

Orange Bread

BILL PURVIANCE, DRIVER

6 small oranges
½ cup canola oil
2 cups sugar
4 large eggs
½ teaspoon vanilla extract
4 cups flour
1 teaspoon baking soda
2 teaspoons baking powder
½ teaspoon salt
1 cup milk
1 cup orange juice

Preheat the oven to 375°F. Place the whole oranges in a pot, cover with 2 quarts water, and boil for about 7 minutes. The oranges must be submerged during boiling. Cut the oranges in half and scoop out the pulp. Discard the pulp and reserve the shells. Cut the orange shells into thin slivers and set aside. In a mixing bowl, blend together the oil and sugar until smooth. Add the eggs, one at a time, and stir until smooth. Stir in the vanilla. In a separate bowl, sift together the flour, bak-

ing soda, baking powder, and salt. Add to the sugar mixture, a few tablespoons at a time, alternating with milk and orange juice, ending with flour mixture. Fold in the orange slivers. Turn into 2 greased 9 by 5-inch loaf pans and bake for 1¼ hours until the bread springs back when lightly touched. Cool in pans before removing to wire racks to cool completely.

Makes 2 loaves

Poppy Seed Bread

NANCY GOODMAN ILAND, FOODSTYLIST

1 cup plus 2 tablespoons sugar
3⅓ cups flour
4 teaspoons baking powder
¼ teaspoon salt
⅓ cup plus 1 tablespoon
poppy seeds
1 cup plus 2 tablespoons oil
1½ cups milk
1½ teaspoons vanilla extract
3 large eggs

Preheat the oven to 350°F. Combine the sugar, flour, baking powder, salt, and poppy seeds in a large bowl and blend well. Mix together the oil, milk, vanilla, and eggs in another bowl. Add the dry ingredients to the liquid ingredients. Mix with an electric mixer at medium speed until smooth, about 4 minutes, scraping the sides of the bowl often. Pour into two 8½ by 4½-inch greased and wax paper-lined loaf pans. Bake for 1 hour and 25 minutes, or until a toothpick comes out clean.

Makes 2 loaves

Zucchini Bread

NANCY GOODMAN ILAND, FOODSTYLIST

3 large eggs, lightly beaten
1 cup vegetable oil
1½ cups light or dark brown sugar
½ cup sugar
2 cups peeled, sliced, and chopped zucchini
2 teaspoons vanilla extract
3 cups flour
1 teaspoon baking soda
1 teaspoon baking powder
1 teaspoon salt
3 teaspoons ground cinnamon
½ cup chopped walnuts
½ cup raisins
½ cup granola

Preheat the oven to 325°F. In a blender or food processor, mix the eggs, oil, sugars, zucchini, and vanilla together. In a bowl, mix together the flour, baking soda, baking powder, salt, cinnamon, walnuts, and raisins. Slowly blend the flour mixture into the egg mixture. Pour into a loaf pan and top with granola. Bake for 1 hour. Cool before serving.

Makes 2 loaves

Peanut Butter and Jelly Sandwich

PHIL ROSE, KEY GRIP

2 tablespoons peanut butter
2 slices wheat, raisin, or white bread
2 tablespoons jelly, any type

Spread peanut butter on one slice of the bread. Spread jelly on the other slice of bread and stick the two pieces together.

Makes 1 serving

Ten

Desserts

"One of the best parts about acting is getting the chance to create lives so different from our own. On the episode 'A Death in Hong Kong,' I played the matriarch of a fabulously wealthy Chinese family living in Hong Kong. I got to wear the most exquisite clothes and to walk up the grandest of staircases feeling like Scarlett O'Hara. In one scene, we were all seated at a luncheon and I glanced down at the beautiful china and discovered that it was authentic. What a classy show and no wonder I felt so royal."

—France Nuyen, actress

Avocado Pie

KIM AND SHERRY KIRSHBAUM, PAINTERS

2 avocados, peeled, seeded, and
   mashed
½ cup fresh lemon juice or fresh
   lime juice
1 can (5 ounces) sweetened
   condensed milk
1 (9-inch) piecrust, baked
1 cup Cool Whip nondairy topping

*I*n a small bowl mix together the avocados, lemon juice or lime juice, and condensed milk. Spoon into the baked piecrust and top with Cool Whip. Chill 3 to 4 hours.

Makes 8 servings

Chocolate Meringue Pie

JULIE ADAMS, ACTRESS

2 tablespoons flour
2 tablespoons cocoa
1 cup sugar
3 large eggs, separated
1 cup condensed milk
4 tablespoons butter or margarine
2 teaspoons vanilla extract
1 (9-inch) piecrust, baked
¼ teaspoon cream of tartar
4 tablespoons sugar

*P*reheat the oven to 400°F. In a medium bowl, mix together the flour, cocoa, and sugar. Add the egg yolks. Beat well and add the milk. Add the butter or margarine and vanilla. Cook in the top of a double boiler until very thick, stirring often. Cool slightly and pour into the baked piecrust. In a small bowl, beat together the egg whites, cream of tartar, and sugar until peaks form. Pour over the filling in piecrust. Bake for 8 to 10 minutes.

Makes 8 servings

Cream Cheese Pie

DOTTIE MOREY, EXECUTIVE PRODUCTION ASSISTANT

12 graham crackers, finely
  crumbled
¼ cup melted butter
2 cups sugar
12 ounces cream cheese, softened
2 large eggs, beaten
3 teaspoons vanilla extract
½ teaspoon fresh lemon juice
1 cup sour cream

Mix together the cracker crumbs, butter, and ½ cup of the sugar. Pat into a 9-inch pie plate. Preheat the oven to 350°F. Combine the cream cheese, eggs, ¾ cup sugar, 2 teaspoons of the vanilla, and the lemon juice and mix with an electric mixer until light and frothy. Pour into the graham cracker crust and bake for 15 to 20 minutes. While the pie bakes, blend the sour cream with remaining sugar and the remaining 1 teaspoon vanilla. Remove the pie from the oven and let cool for 5 minutes. Spread the sour cream topping smoothly over the pie. Return to the oven and bake for 10 minutes longer. Chill for at least 5 hours before serving.

Makes 12 servings

Mama's Cream Pie

GRETCHEN GERMAN, ACTRESS

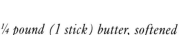

⅓ cup flour
½ cup sugar
¼ teaspoon salt
2 cups milk, scalded
3 egg yolks, beaten
2 tablespoons butter
½ teaspoon vanilla extract
1 (9-inch) piecrust, baked
½ pint heavy cream, whipped

Mix together the flour, sugar, and salt. Gradually add the milk. Cook in the top of a double boiler until thick, stirring constantly. Add the egg yolks gradually. Cook for 2 minutes, then let cool. Add the butter and vanilla. Pour the mixture into the baked piecrust. Top with freshly whipped cream. As a variation, try lining the bottom of the piecrust with 2 sliced bananas before adding the filling, or add 1 cup shredded coconut to the filling mixture.

Makes 8 servings

French Silk Pie

KATHERINE WALLACE, EXECUTIVE ASSISTANT TO MS. LANSBURY

¼ pound (1 stick) butter, softened
¾ cup sugar
2 squares unsweetened chocolate, melted and cooled
1 teaspoon vanilla extract
2 large eggs
1 (9-inch) graham cracker crust
1 cup whipping cream, whipped

Cream together the butter and sugar. Blend in the melted chocolate and vanilla. Add 1 egg and beat for 5 minutes. Add the second egg and beat for another 5 minutes. It is important to beat for the full amount of time to make sure all the sugar is dissolved and the filling is light. Pour the mixture into the piecrust and chill for at least 2 hours. Top with freshly whipped cream.

Makes 8 servings

Fudge Pie

MADLYN RHUE, ACTRESS

1 cup sugar
¼ pound (1 stick) butter, softened
2 large eggs, separated
2 ounces dark chocolate, melted
½ cup all-purpose flour, sifted
1 teaspoon vanilla extract
⅓ teaspoon salt

Preheat the oven to 325°F. In a mixing bowl, blend the sugar and butter until creamy. Beat in the egg yolks. Add the chocolate. Blend in the flour and vanilla. In a separate bowl, whip the egg whites with the salt until stiff and fold into the batter. Pour the batter into a greased 8-inch pie plate. Bake for 1 hour. Serve with vanilla ice cream and whipped cream, if desired.

Makes 8 servings

Key Lime Pie

JESSICA WALTER, ACTRESS

2 cans (5 ounces each) sweetened
  condensed milk
½ cup fresh lime juice or fresh
  lemon juice (key limes taste best)
3 egg yolks
1 (9-inch) graham cracker crust
1 pint heavy cream, whipped

Blend the condensed milk, lime juice, and egg yolks well. Pour into the graham cracker crust. Chill 2 hours. Top with whipped cream before serving. It will be easier to squeeze all the juice out of the limes or lemons if they are rolled on the countertop before cutting.

Makes 8 servings

Upside-Down Lemon Meringue Pie

BRUCE GRAY, ACTOR

3 large eggs, separated
1½ cups sugar
½ teaspoon cream of tartar
(omit if you beat the egg
whites in a copper bowl)
3 tablespoons fresh lemon juice
2 teaspoons finely grated
lemon rind
1 cup whipping cream

*P*reheat the oven to 300°F. Beat the egg whites until fluffy. Gradually add 1 cup of the sugar and the cream of tartar. Continue beating until peaks are stiff but not dry. Shape into a greased 9-inch pie plate. Bake for 40 minutes. Let cool completely in the oven.

In the top of a double boiler, beat the egg yolks, gradually adding the remaining ½ cup sugar, lemon juice, and lemon rind. Cook, beating constantly, until slightly thickened, then let cool. Whip the cream until soft peaks form and fold into the egg mixture. Pour the mixture over the cooled pie. Chill for 24 hours before serving.

Makes 8 servings

Strawberry Pie with Glaze

BARBARA MCHUGH, SET WARDROBE

1 cup sugar
3 tablespoons cornstarch
1 tablespoon fresh lemon juice
3 pints fresh strawberries, sliced
1 (9-inch) piecrust, baked
16 ounces cream cheese, softened
2 cups whipped cream (optional)

*I*n a saucepan, combine the sugar, cornstarch, lemon juice, and 1 pint of the strawberries. Cook over low heat for ½ hour or until thickened, stirring constantly. This will be the glaze over the strawberry filling. Line the bottom of the piecrust with the cream cheese. Arrange the remaining strawberries on top of the cream cheese then pour the glaze over the bed of strawberries. Chill for at least 2 hours. If desired, serve topped with whipped cream.

Makes 6 to 8 servings

Chocolate Bourbon Pecan Pie

EFRAIN FIGUEROA, ACTOR

¾ cup sugar
2 tablespoons flour
½ teaspoon salt
1 cup dark corn syrup
2 large eggs, lightly beaten
¼ cup evaporated milk
1 teaspoon vanilla extract
1 cup pecans
1 cup semisweet chocolate chips
¼ cup bourbon
1 (9-inch) piecrust

Preheat the oven to 375°F. Mix the sugar, flour, and salt. Mix in the corn syrup, then add the eggs, evaporated milk, and vanilla. Stir until smooth. Add the pecans, chocolate chips, and bourbon and mix well. Pour into the piecrust and bake in the center of the oven for 1 hour. Check after 40 minutes and cover loosely with foil if the top is too brown. Serve at room temperature or slightly warm topped with whipped cream.

Makes 10 servings

Sour Cream Raisin Pie

CAROLE CHRISTOPHER, PRODUCTION ASSISTANT

1 cup raisins
3 large eggs, separated
1 teaspoon cornstarch
1 teaspoon butter
½ cup sour cream
½ cup milk
1½ cups sugar
Salt to taste
1 teaspoon vanilla extract
1 (9-inch) piecrust

Preheat the oven to 425°F. Cook the raisins in 2 cups water until soft, about 15 minutes. Let cool. Add the egg yolks, cornstarch, butter, sour cream, milk, 1 cup of the sugar, and salt. Cook over low heat until blended. The mixture will thicken as it heats. Add the vanilla, stir, let cool slightly, and pour into the piecrust. Beat the egg whites until foamy. Add the remaining ½ cup sugar and beat until the mixture forms stiff peaks. Spoon over the pie. Bake for 3 to 10 minutes until light brown. Do not overbake. Let cool before cutting.

Makes 8 servings

Pecan Pie

SUZANNE WAITE, SCRIPT SUPERVISOR

½ cup light or dark brown sugar
2 tablespoons butter, softened
2 large eggs, lightly beaten
2 tablespoons flour
¼ teaspoon salt
1 teaspoon vanilla extract
1 cup dark corn syrup
1½ cups pecan halves
1 (9-inch) piecrust, unbaked

Preheat the oven to 350°F. Cream together the brown sugar, butter, eggs, flour, salt, vanilla, and corn syrup. Beat well and stir in the pecans. Pour the mixture into the piecrust and bake ½ hour to 40 minutes or until the filling is set. Do not overbake. The nuts will float to the surface of the filling during baking.

Makes 8 servings

Cream Puffs

VINCE BORGESE, PROP MAN

¼ pound (1 stick) butter
1 cup sifted flour
4 large eggs

Preheat the oven to 400°F. Boil the butter in 1 cup water. Add the flour and stir constantly over moderate heat until it leaves the sides of the pan. Remove from heat. Let the mixture cool slightly: beat in the eggs, one at a time, making sure the mixture is smooth before each addition. Drop by the spoonful onto a greased cookie sheet about 2 inches apart, allowing plenty of room for expansion. Bake for ½ hour or until golden brown. To test, cut the top from one puff. If the inside is soft and sticky, continue baking until the inside tests dry and crisp. Avoid opening the oven until the cream puffs are done. If desired, fill the puffs with about 1 teaspoon of any filling, such as whipped cream or vanilla pudding. Sprinkle confectioners' sugar over tops and serve.

Makes 12 servings

Quick Apple Crisp

ZANNE SHAW, STAND-IN TO MS. LANSBURY

1 can (21 ounces) apple pie filling
¾ cup light or dark brown sugar
½ cup all-purpose flour
½ cup quick-cooking or
* old-fashioned oats*
⅓ cup butter or margarine
¾ teaspoon ground cinnamon
½ teaspoon ground nutmeg

Preheat the oven to 375°F. Place the apple pie filling in a 1-quart baking dish. In a small bowl, combine all the remaining ingredients. Sprinkle over the apples and bake for ½ hour or until the topping is golden brown. Serve warm topped with vanilla ice cream, if desired.

Makes 4 to 6 servings

Microwave Apple Dessert

ZANNE SHAW, STAND-IN TO MS. LANSBURY

4 tablespoons butter or margarine,
* melted*
½ cup graham cracker crumbs
½ cup quick-cooking oats
2 tablespoons packed light or dark
* brown sugar*
2 tablespoons all-purpose flour
1 teaspoon ground cinnamon
2 pounds Granny Smith apples,
* peeled, cored and thinly sliced*
* (about 6 cups)*
¼ cup sugar

Make the topping by blending together the butter, graham cracker crumbs, oats, brown sugar, flour, and cinnamon. Set aside. Combine the apples and sugar in an 8-inch square microwave-safe baking dish: toss to mix. Sprinkle the graham cracker topping evenly over the apples. Microwave uncovered on HIGH for 8 to 10 minutes or until the apples are tender when pierced, rotating the dish once. Let cool directly on a heatproof surface for ½ hour until topping is firm.

Makes 6 servings

Easy Cherry Cobbler

GEORGE ZIMMERMAN, DRIVER CO-CAPTAIN

1 teaspoon almond extract
2 cans (21 ounces each) cherry pie filling
1 box (12½ ounces) yellow cake mix
3 tablespoons butter or margarine, melted

Preheat the oven to 350°F. Mix the almond extract into the cherry filling and spread evenly into a 3-quart baking dish. Sprinkle the cake mix evenly over the top. Drizzle the melted butter over the cake mix, covering thoroughly. Bake for 35 to 40 minutes. This is great topped with whipped cream or ice cream.

Makes 8 servings

Fresh Peach Cobbler

ROBIN BEAUCHESNE, MAKEUP ARTIST

2 pounds fresh peaches, sliced (about 4 cups)
1¼ cups plus 2 tablespoons sugar
2 tablespoons butter
3 teaspoons ground cinnamon
1½ cups flour
2 teaspoons baking powder
¾ teaspoon salt
3 tablespoons vegetable shortening
½ cup milk

To make the filling: Preheat the oven to 400°F. Combine the peaches, 1¼ cups of the sugar, butter, and 2 teaspoons of the cinnamon in an ungreased baking dish. Place in the oven for 15 minutes to heat until the dough for the crust is ready.

To make the crust: In a mixing bowl, combine the flour, 1 tablespoon of the sugar, baking powder, salt, and remaining 1 teaspoon cinnamon. Cut in the shortening and add the milk. Mix until the dough forms a ball. Drop by spoonfuls onto the hot peaches. Sprinkle with remaining 1 tablespoon sugar. Bake for 25 minutes to ½ hour or until the dough is lightly brown.

Makes 8 servings

Cream Cheese Flan

EFRAIN FIGUEROA, ACTOR

1 cup sugar
4 to 6 ounces cream cheese, softened
2 cans (5 ounces each) evaporated milk
1¾ cups milk
2 cans (5 ounces each) condensed milk
1 teaspoon vanilla extract
3 large eggs
1 can (12 ounces) grated coconut in syrup (found in Spanish supermarkets)

Preheat the oven to 375°F. In a skillet, melt the sugar with ¼ cup water until the sugar turns golden brown. Swirl the pan occasionally, but do not stir. Immediately pour into a ring mold or an 8-inch square ovenproof dish: coat the bottom and sides by tilting the mold or dish. Set aside on a rack to cool. In a bowl, mix together the cream cheese, evaporated milk, milk, condensed milk, vanilla, and eggs. If desired, use 6 ounces of cream cheese instead of 4; the more cream cheese, the denser the flan will be. Mix well and pour into the mold or ovenproof dish on top of the caramelized sugar. Place the mold or dish in a large roasting pan in the center of the oven. Carefully pour hot water into the roasting pan around the mold until it reaches halfway up the sides. Bake for 1 hour (10 to 15 minutes longer if you like the flan firmer.) Remove the flan from the oven and cool on a metal rack. Once cool, cover tightly with plastic wrap and chill for at least 4 hours or overnight. To serve, run a knife around the edge of the flan (between the flan and the mold) and invert onto a platter big enough to keep the caramel syrup from overflowing. Top with coconut, if desired, or garnish with strawberries tossed with sliced almonds and ½ cup amaretto. Serve with whipped cream on the side.

Makes 8 to 10 servings

Sweet Potato Flan

BRUCE GRAY, ACTOR

1 package (1½ ounces) flan mix
(Jell-O, Royal, or Knorr brand)
2 cups milk
1 can (14 ounces) sweetened
condensed milk
1 can (9 ounces) sweet potatoes
or yams, with syrup

lace the caramel syrup from the flan mix in a 2-quart ceramic or shallow glass bowl. Cook the flan mix with the milk and condensed milk until boiling, stirring constantly, about 10 minutes. Remove from heat and set aside. Purée the sweet potatoes or yams in a blender, using the syrup from the can to make a thick, smooth mixture. Add to the cooked flan mix. Pour into the bowl containing the caramel syrup. Chill for at least 5 hours or overnight. Invert on a serving dish to serve.

Makes 6 servings

Rice Pudding

SHARON WALDMAN, PRODUCTION ASSISTANT

2 cups cooked Minute Rice
1 cup sugar
2 teaspoons butter
3 large eggs, lightly beaten
1 can (5 ounces) condensed milk
2 teaspoons vanilla extract
½ teaspoon ground nutmeg
½ teaspoon ground cinnamon

reheat the oven to 350°F. Mix together all the ingredients, reserving a little nutmeg and cinnamon to sprinkle on top. Pour into a baking dish. Set the baking dish in a pan of hot water and bake 20 minutes to ½ hour or until the rice thickens to the desired consistency. Sprinkle with nutmeg and cinnamon and serve warm.

Makes 8 servings

Créme Caramel

FRANCE NUYEN, ACTRESS

¼ cup plus 3 tablespoons sugar
2 cups milk
3 large eggs
¼ teaspoon salt
1 teaspoon vanilla extract

Preheat the oven to 350°F. Mix 3 tablespoons of the sugar with 1 teaspoon water and pour into a fluted metal flan mold. Protect your hands with gloves and tip and rotate the mold over a flame so the melted sugar coats the bottom of the mold and halfway up the sides. Cook the mold in the oven until the caramel turns dark brown; do not let it burn. Remove from the oven and set aside. Mix together the remaining ¼ cup sugar, milk, eggs, salt, and vanilla in a bowl. Pour into the mold. Place the mold in a shallow pan filled with about 1½ inches of water and bake for 40 minutes. Test after 35 minutes by inserting a knife into the center. If it comes out clean, the dessert is done. If not, cook for another 5 to 10 minutes. Cool and invert onto a serving plate. Serve with whipped cream.

Makes 6 to 8 servings

Low-Fat Peach Banana Bread Pudding

MELINDA VILLARREAL, SET DRESSING

8 slices fat-free whole wheat bread, cut into 1-inch cubes (about 3½ cups)
1½ cups evaporated skim milk
4 egg whites, lightly beaten
½ cup frozen apple juice concentrate, thawed
1 can (16 ounces) juice-packed peaches, chopped
2 ripe bananas, sliced
1 teaspoon fresh lemon juice
1½ teaspoons ground cinnamon
1⅔ teaspoons ground nutmeg
⅓ cup pure maple syrup
1½ teaspoons vanilla extract

*P*reheat the oven to 325°F. In a large bowl, mix all the ingredients together well. Pour into a 2-quart ovenproof baking dish. Bake for 1 hour, or until a knife inserted in the center comes out clean. Cool slightly and serve warm or cold.

Makes 8 to 10 servings

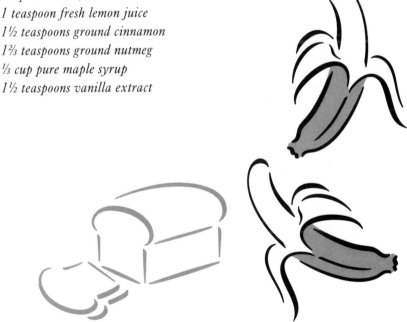

Haupia (Traditional Luau Dessert)

TAMLYN TOMITA, ACTRESS

1½ cups coconut milk
1½ cups water
½ cup plus 2 tablespoons sugar
½ cup plus 2 tablespoons cornstarch

Combine all the ingredients in a saucepan. Stir over medium heat until thickened. Lower heat and cook for 10 minutes, stirring constantly to avoid lumping or burning. Pour into an 8-inch square dish and chill until set. Cut into squares.

Makes 20 servings

Holiday Trifle

PAULINE BRAILSFORD, ACTRESS

2 cups raspberry jam
2 packages (12 ounces each)
   ladyfingers
1 cup medium-dry sherry
½ cup toasted almond slivers
3 cups fresh raspberries or
   2 packages (12 ounces each)
   frozen raspberries
4 cups egg custard, homemade or
   made from instant custard powder
1 pint whipping cream, whipped

Spread the jam over the ladyfingers and layer them in a glass dish. Pour the sherry over the dish and soak at least 4 hours or overnight. Sprinkle with almonds. Layer the raspberries over the ladyfingers, then layer the custard. Before serving, top with whipped cream and decorate with almonds.

Makes 12 servings

Persimmon Pudding

KATHERINE CANNON, ACTRESS

4 large, very ripe Japanese fuyu
  persimmons
3 large eggs
1¼ cups sugar
1½ cups all-purpose flour
1 teaspoon baking powder
1 teaspoon baking soda
½ teaspoon salt
¼ pound (1 stick) butter, melted
2½ cups evaporated milk
2 teaspoons ground cinnamon
1 teaspoon ground ginger
½ teaspoon freshly grated nutmeg
1 cup chopped pecans (optional)

*P*reheat the oven to 325°F. Strain the persimmons through a colander or sieve to create 2 cups of pulp from the juicy flesh. Place the pulp in a mixing bowl and beat in the remaining ingredients by hand. Pour the mixture into a greased 9-inch square baking dish. Bake for 1 hour, until firm. Serve warm with a rich vanilla ice cream.

Makes 8 servings

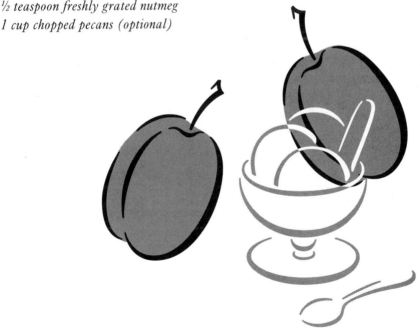

Mexican Natillas

PAUL CONTI, COMPUTER GRAPHICS

4 large eggs, separated
¼ cup flour
4 cups milk
¾ cups sugar
1 teaspoon fresh Mexican vanilla
 or vanilla extract
Ground nutmeg to taste
Ground cinnamon to taste

Place the eggs yolks, flour, and 1 cup of the milk in a bowl and stir to a paste. Set aside. Place the remaining milk and the sugar in a medium saucepan and scald over medium heat. Add the egg yolk mixture to the saucepan and continue to cook until it becomes a soft custard. Add the vanilla. Beat the egg whites until stiff peaks form and fold into the custard. Pour into serving glasses and chill for 2 hours. Garnish with cinnamon and nutmeg.

Makes 8 servings

Rugelach

NANCY GOODMAN ILAND, FOODSTYLIST

½ pound (2 stick) butter, softened
8 ounces cream cheese, softened
2 cups flour
1 cup apricot or pineapple
 preserves
½ cup chopped nuts, any type

Mix together the butter, cream cheese, and flour. Chill for ½ hour. Preheat the oven to 350°F. Knead, roll out, and cut the dough into 3-inch triangles. Fill each triangle with a dab of preserves and chopped nuts. Pull the 3 corners together and pinch to hold. Bake for 12 to 18 minutes in an ungreased pan.

Makes 3 to 4 dozen

Raspberry Créme Brûlée

TAMLYN TOMITA, ACTRESS

3 cups half-and-half
1 cup heavy cream
1 vanilla bean, halved lengthwise
5 large eggs
4 egg yolks
½ cup sugar
1 pint fresh raspberries
¼ cup packed light brown sugar

*I*n a medium saucepan, combine the half-and-half with cream and vanilla bean. Scald over medium heat for 5 minutes. Remove from heat, cover, and set aside. Preheat the oven to 325°F. In a large bowl, whisk together the eggs, yolks, and sugar. Slowly add the hot half-and-half mixture, stirring constantly until well blended. Strain into a 1½-quart ovenproof baking dish. Place the dish in a slightly larger baking pan and pour enough hot water into the pan to reach halfway up the side of the dish. Bake in the center of the oven for 1 hour, until a toothpick inserted near the edge comes out clean. Remove from the oven and let cool completely in a water bath for about 1 hour. Cover and chill for at least 3 hours. Preheat the broiler. Stuff the raspberries, one by one, into the custard. Sift the brown sugar over the top, completely covering the surface. Broil about 6 inches from the heat source, turning occasionally, for 2 to 3 minutes, until the sugar has melted and caramelized. Chill for 10 minutes before serving.

Makes 8 servings

Raspberries Frangipane

STEVE FORREST, ACTOR

6 egg yolks
½ cup plus 3 tablespoons sugar
⅛ teaspoon salt
⅓ cup flour
2½ cups milk
2-inch piece of vanilla bean
2½ tablespoons butter
12 macaroons, coarsely crumbled
1 pint whipping cream
¼ cup kirsch
2½ pints raspberries

*I*n a large bowl beat together the egg yolks, ½ cup of the sugar and the salt with a wire whisk, until light in color. Whisk in the flour. Meanwhile, scald the milk with the vanilla bean. Then gradually add the milk to the egg mixture while whisking fast. Open the vanilla bean and scrape the seeds into the custard. Discard the bean. Pour the custard into a saucepan and cook over low heat, stirring constantly, until the custard is very thick. Remove from heat and add the butter and macaroons. Turn the custard into a 3-quart glass dish and cover with a buttered piece of wax paper. Chill several hours or overnight until cold. Before serving, whip the cream with the kirsch and the remaining 3 tablespoons sugar. Serve topped with the raspberries and whipped cream.

Makes 12 servings

White Chocolate Mousse with Fresh Raspberry Sauce

PAUL CONTI, COMPUTER GRAPHICS

6 egg yolks
1⅓ cups chopped white chocolate, melted
1 cup heavy cream, whipped
1 cup fresh raspberries
1 teaspoon fresh lemon juice
Sugar to taste

To make the mousse: In the top of a double boiler over low heat, beat the egg yolks with ¼ cup cold water until thickened. Transfer to a large bowl. Add the white chocolate. Fold in the whipped cream. Chill for 3 hours. Use a pastry bag to fill dessert or wine glasses with the mousse.

To make the sauce: Mix the raspberries with the lemon juice in a blender. Add sugar to taste. Gently pour over the mousse. Garnish with fresh mint leaves and serve.

Makes 6 to 8 servings

Rum Cake

MONTEY F. MENAPACE, SET LIGHTING TECHNICIAN

1 cup chopped pecans or walnuts
1 box (18 ounces) yellow cake
  mix (see Note)
4 large eggs
½ cup vegetable oil
1 cup dark 80-proof rum
½ teaspoon rum extract
1 package (3¼ ounces) vanilla
  instant pudding mix
½ pound (2 sticks) butter
1 cup sugar

*P*reheat the oven to 325°F. Grease and flour a 10-inch tube or a 12-cup Bundt pan. Sprinkle the nuts over the bottom of the pan. Combine the cake mix, eggs, ½ cup cold water, vegetable oil, ½ cup of the rum, rum extract, and pudding mix. Mix well. Pour the batter over the pecans and bake for 1 hour. While the cake bakes, make the glaze. Melt the butter in a saucepan. Stir in ¼ cup cold water and the sugar. Boil for 5 minutes, stirring constantly. Remove from heat. Stir in the remaining ½ cup rum. When the cake is done, cool, invert on a plate, and prick the top several times with a fork. Spoon and brush the glaze over the top and sides of the cake until all the glaze is used.

Note: If using yellow cake mix with pudding already in the mix, omit instant pudding and use 3 large eggs instead of 4, and ⅓ cup vegetable oil instead of ½ cup.

Makes 10 servings

Caramel Cake

ERIC WOODALL, ACTOR

½ cup butter or margarine, softened

½ cup vegetable shortening, softened

2 cups extra-fine granulated sugar

4 large eggs, at room temperature

3 cups sifted cake flour

2½ teaspoons baking powder

¼ teaspoon salt

1 cup milk, at room temperature

1 teaspoon vanilla extract

1 teaspoon lemon flavoring

*P*reheat the oven to 350°F. In a large mixing bowl, cream together the butter and shortening. Gradually add the sugar, creaming until light and fluffy. Add the eggs, one at a time, beating well after each addition. In a separate bowl, sift the flour, baking powder, and salt together. Add the flour mixture to the bowl with the eggs. Add milk, vanilla, and lemon flavoring. Mix thoroughly with an electric mixer. Bake in 3 greased and floured 9-inch layer pans for 25 minutes to ½ hour. Do not open the oven door during baking. When done, let cool in pans for 10 minutes. Remove from pans and layer, putting a coat of Caramel Icing (recipe follows) between the layers and using the remaining icing to cover the top and sides.

Makes 10 to 12 servings

Caramel Icing

ERIC WOODALL, ACTOR

¼ pound (1 stick) butter or
  margarine
1 cup packed light brown sugar
¼ cup milk
1¾ cups sifted confectioners' sugar
1 teaspoon vanilla extract

Melt the butter or margarine in a heavy saucepan. Add the brown sugar and cook over low heat for 2 minutes. Stir in the milk. Bring to a full rolling boil. Remove from heat and put the saucepan in a pan of ice water until cool enough to hold in your hand (about 2 minutes). Stir in the confectioners' sugar and beat until thickened. Add the vanilla and spread over the top and sides of the Caramel Cake (preceding recipe) or your choice of cake.

Makes 2 cups: enough to frost one 9-inch layer cake

Chocolate Chip Sour Cream Coffee Cake

ANTHONY SHAW, DIRECTOR

½ pound (2 sticks) margarine,
  softened
1¼ cups sugar
3 large eggs, separated
1 cup sour cream
1¾ cups flour
1 teaspoon baking powder
1 teaspoon ground cinnamon

Preheat the oven to 325°F. Cream together the margarine and 1 cup sugar. Add the egg yolks and sour cream and beat until light and fluffy. Mix in the flour and baking powder. Beat the egg whites until stiff peaks form and add to the mixture. Pour half the mixture into a greased Bundt pan. Sprinkle the remaining ¼ cup sugar, cinnamon, pecans,

½ cup chopped pecans
2 cups chocolate chips
Confectioners' sugar

and chocolate chips on top of the batter. Pour the remaining half of the batter over inside ingredients. Bake for 1 hour. Sprinkle with confectioners' sugar when done.

Makes 8 to 10 servings

Crumb Cake with Topping

THOMAS RYAN, ACTOR

½ pound plus 4 tablespoons
  (2½ sticks) butter, softened
  (do not substitute margarine)
4 cups flour
½ cup dark brown sugar
1½ teaspoons ground cinnamon
¾ cup sugar
1 teaspoon vanilla extract
2 large eggs
1 tablespoon baking powder
¾ cup milk
¼ cup confectioners' sugar

Preheat the oven to 350°F. Line a 9 by 12-inch pan with aluminum foil. In a mixing bowl, combine 12 tablespoons of the butter, 2 cups of the flour, the brown sugar, and the cinnamon. Mix until crumbly and set aside. In a medium pan, cream the remaining 8 tablespoons butter and the sugar. Add the vanilla, mix in the eggs, and blend well. Sift together the remaining 2 cups flour and the baking powder and add to the mixture. Add the milk. Beat the batter only until the ingredients are well mixed. Pour evenly into the lined pan. Spread the topping over the cake batter and bake for 40 to 50 minutes. Let cool. When cooled, sprinkle the confectioners' sugar over the top.

Makes 10 to 12 servings

Gingerbread

LITA ISUMU, SET PAINTER

¼ pound butter, melted
1 cup sugar
2 large eggs
¾ cup boiling water
¾ cup light molasses
2½ cups flour
2 teaspoons baking soda
½ teaspoon salt
2 teaspoons ground ginger

Preheat the oven to 350°F. Grease and lightly flour a 9-inch square cake pan. Mix together the butter and sugar and beat until creamy. Add the eggs and beat well. Add the boiling water and molasses and blend. In a separate bowl, mix together the flour, baking soda, salt, and ginger. Add to the first mixture and combine thoroughly. Pour into the pan and bake for 35 to 45 minutes until a toothpick inserted in the center comes out clean. Cool in the pan for about 5 minutes before putting on a plate. This is great served with whipped cream.

Makes 8 servings

Pear Gingerbread with Caramel Sauce

FREDDIE MILLER, BOOM MAN

2½ cups sifted all-purpose flour, plus extra for dusting
1 teaspoon baking soda
1¼ teaspoons ground ginger
1 teaspoon ground cinnamon
½ teaspoon ground nutmeg
½ teaspoon ground mace
¼ teaspoon salt

Preheat the oven to 375°F. Grease and flour a 3-quart baking pan. Sift together the flour, baking soda, ginger, cinnamon, nutmeg, mace, and salt into a bowl and set aside. Put ½ pound of the butter in a large bowl and beat with an electric mixer on high until smooth, scraping down sides as necessary with a rubber spatula. Add the sugar and eggs

208

¾ pound (3 sticks) butter, softened

1 cup sugar

3 large eggs

1 cup light molasses

¾ cup hot water

1½ cups peeled, seeded, and diced
  pears

1 cup packed light or dark brown
  sugar

1 cup whipping cream

and beat about 5 minutes longer until the mixture is light and fluffy. Reduce mixer speed to low and gradually beat in the molasses and hot water. Add the flour mixture, a small amount at a time, beating just until the batter is smooth and all the dry ingredients are moistened. Use a rubber spatula to stir in the pear pieces. Pour into the prepared baking pan. Place in the middle of the oven and bake for 35 to 40 minutes or until a toothpick inserted in the center comes out clean. Place the pan on a wire rack and cool for 10 to 15 minutes. Cut into squares.

While the cake bakes, make the caramel sauce. In a medium saucepan, combine the brown sugar, whipping cream, and the remaining ¼ pound butter and bring to a boil. Boil over medium heat for 5 minutes, stirring occasionally. Remove from heat and cool to room temperature. Spoon about 2 tablespoons of sauce onto each serving plate. Place squares of cake on the sauce and serve.

Makes 12 servings

Pumpkin Cake

SHARON WALDMAN, PRODUCTION ASSISTANT

3 cups flour, sifted
3 cups sugar
1 teaspoon baking soda
¼ teaspoon salt
½ teaspoon baking powder
1 teaspoon ground cloves
1 teaspoon ground nutmeg
1 teaspoon ground cinnamon
1 teaspoon ground allspice
1 can (15 ounces) pumpkin pie
  filling
1 cup vegetable oil
3 large eggs, beaten
1 teaspoon vanilla extract

Preheat the oven to 350°F. Grease and flour a Bundt pan. Combine the flour, sugar, baking soda, salt, baking powder, and spices in a mixing bowl and blend thoroughly. Set aside. Combine the pumpkin, oil, eggs, and vanilla in a separate bowl and beat thoroughly with a fork. Add the liquid ingredients to the dry ones and mix together, by hand or with an electric mixer, until well blended. Pour batter into Bundt pan. Bake for ½ hour to 45 minutes, until springy to the touch or until a toothpick inserted in the cake comes out clean. Cool the pan on a rack for 15 minutes, then turn the cake out onto the rack to cool completely. Frost or sprinkle with confectioners' sugar, if desired.

Makes 8 to 10 servings

Hummingbird Cake

GEORGE DYE, FIRST ASSISTANT CAMERA

3 cups flour
2 cups sugar
1 teaspoon salt
1 teaspoon baking soda
3 large eggs, beaten
1½ cups mild-tasting oil
1½ teaspoons vanilla extract
1 can (8 ounces) crushed
   pineapple, drained
1¼ pounds bananas, mashed
   (about 2 cups)
2 cups chopped pecans
1 teaspoon ground cinnamon

Preheat the oven to 350°F. Combine the flour, sugar, salt, and baking soda in a large bowl. Add the eggs and oil, and stir until the dry ingredients are moistened. Do not beat. Stir in the vanilla, pineapple, bananas, and nuts. Spoon the batter into 3 greased and floured 9-inch cake pans. Bake for 25 minutes to ½ hour. Cool in pans for 10 minutes, then remove from the pans and cool completely. Spread each layer with Cream Cheese Frosting (recipe follows), assemble the layers, and cover the top and sides with the remaining frosting.

Makes 10 servings

Cream Cheese Frosting

GEORGE DYE, FIRST ASSISTANT CAMERA

8 ounces cream cheese, softened
¼ pound (1 stick) butter, softened
2 cups confectioners' sugar
1 teaspoon vanilla extract

Cream together the cream cheese and but-ter until smooth. Add the confectioners' sugar and beat until light and fluffy. Stir in the vanilla. Serve on Hummingbird Cake (preceding recipe) or with the cake of your choice.

Makes 2 cups: enough to frost one 9-inch layer cake

Lemon Pudding Poppy Seed Cake

BRUCE KNECHTGES, SPECIAL EFFECTS

4 large eggs
1 cup canola oil
1 package (3 ounces) instant lemon pudding
1 box (10 ounces) lemon cake mix
5 tablespoons poppy seeds
½ teaspoon almond extract
¼ cup confectioners' sugar

Preheat the oven to 350°F. Combine the eggs, oil, 1 cup water, pudding mix, cake mix, poppy seeds, and almond extract. Blend with an electric mixer for 2 minutes. Pour into a Bundt pan and bake for 45 to 55 minutes. When the cake is done, cool, invert, dust with confectioners' sugar, and serve.

Makes 8 to 10 servings

Snippy Doodle Sponge Cake

STEVE KLINGHOFFER, SOUND PLAYBACK

1 tablespoon butter or margarine, softened
1 cup sugar, plus extra for topping
2 large eggs, beaten
2 teaspoons ground cinnamon
1½ teaspoons baking powder
1 cup flour
½ cup milk
Sugar

Preheat the oven to 350°F. Cream together the butter or margarine and sugar. Add the eggs. In a separate bowl, mix the cinnamon and baking powder with the flour. Add to the butter-and-egg mixture. Add the milk. Pour into an 8-inch square pan and bake for 25 minutes until cake springs up when done. Sprinkle top with sugar when cooled. This can be served with a dollop of whipped cream.

Makes 6 to 8 servings

Frosted Lemon Poppy Seed Cake

SARA NELSON, ACTRESS

CAKE

¼ pound (1 stick) butter, softened
2 cups flour
2 teaspoons baking powder
5 large eggs
½ cup plain nonfat yogurt or
  sour cream
1 teaspoon balsamic vinegar
1 teaspoon vanilla extract
Juice of 1 lemon
2 tablespoons grated lemon rind
½ cup poppy seeds

FROSTING

⅓ cup sugar
⅓ cup water
⅓ cup fresh lemon juice
½ cup lemon curd
½ cup brandy
Grated rind of 1 lemon

To make the cake: Preheat the oven to 350°F. In a large bowl, mix together all the cake ingredients until smooth. Pour into a greased and floured Bundt pan and bake for 1 hour. Remove and cool. Top with frosting or fresh whipped cream.

To make the frosting: Mix together the sugar, water, lemon juice, lemon curd, and brandy in a bowl until creamy. Spread over the cooled cake and sprinkle with the grated lemon rind.

Makes 10 servings

Molasses Crumb Cake

SUZANNE GEIGER, SECOND ASSISTANT DIRECTOR

¾ cup flour
½ cup packed light or dark brown
 sugar
2 tablespoons vegetable shortening
⅛ teaspoon ground nutmeg
⅛ teaspoon ground ginger
⅛ teaspoon ground cloves
⅛ teaspoon ground cinnamon
¼ teaspoon salt
½ cup molasses
1 egg yolk, well beaten
½ teaspoon baking soda, dissolved
 in ¾ cup boiling water
1 (9-inch) piecrust, baked

Preheat the oven to 450°F. Combine the flour, brown sugar, shortening, nutmeg, ginger, cloves, cinnamon, and salt. In a separate bowl, combine the molasses, egg yolk, and dissolved baking soda. Pour alternate layers of dry and liquid mixtures into the piecrust, ending with a dry layer. Bake 7 to 10 minutes until the crust edges start to brown. Reduce heat to 350°F and bake 20 minutes longer, until firm.

Makes 10 servings

Oatmeal Chocolate Chip Cookies

FRANK MCNAIR, SECURITY GUARD

½ pound (2 sticks) butter, softened
1 cup sugar
1 cup light or dark brown sugar
2 large eggs, beaten
1 teaspoons vanilla extract
2 cups flour
½ teaspoon salt

Preheat the oven to 375°F. Cream together the butter, sugar, and brown sugar. Add the eggs and vanilla. Mix in the flour, salt, oats, baking powder, and baking soda. Add the chocolate chips, grated chocolate, and nuts. Roll the dough into balls about 1 inch in diameter and place on ungreased cookie

2½ cups old-fashioned oats,
  blended to a fine powder
1 teaspoon baking powder
1 teaspoon baking soda
¾ pound chocolate chips
4 ounces milk chocolate, grated
1½ cups chopped nuts (any type)

sheets, spaced 2 inches apart. Bake for 6 to 8 minutes.

Makes 4 dozen cookies

Philly Pound Cake

TOM MARGOZEWITZ, PROP MAN

8 ounces cream cheese, softened
12 tablespoons (1½ sticks)
  margarine, softened
1⅔ cups sugar
1½ teaspoons vanilla extract
4 large eggs
2 cups sifted cake flour
1½ teaspoons baking powder
¼ cup sifted confectioners' sugar

Preheat the oven to 325°F. Combine the cream cheese, margarine, sugar, and vanilla, mixing until well blended. Add the eggs and mix at low speed with an electric mixer until blended. Sift together the flour and baking powder and add gradually. Mix at low speed until blended. Pour into a greased and floured loaf pan. Bake for 1 hour and 20 minutes. Cool for 5 minutes in the pan. Remove and cool completely on a wire rack. Sprinkle with confectioners' sugar.

Makes 8 servings

Prune Cake

BRUCE KNECHTGES, SPECIAL EFFECTS

12 ounces pitted prunes
¾ pound (3 sticks) butter, softened
1¼ cups sugar
3 large eggs, beaten
1½ teaspoons vanilla extract
3 cups flour
1½ teaspoons ground, sweetened
  chocolate
¾ teaspoon ground nutmeg
¾ teaspoon ground cinnamon
1½ cups plus 3 teaspoons milk
3 teaspoons baking soda

Preheat the oven to 350°F. Add a small amount of water to the prunes and heat in the microwave for 8 minutes, until stewed and softened. Let cool. Drain the excess liquid and reserve. Mash the prunes by hand, adding liquid if necessary. Cream together the butter and sugar. Add the eggs and vanilla. In a separate bowl, mix together the flour, chocolate, nutmeg, and cinnamon. Add 1½ cups milk to the butter mixture. Dissolve the baking soda in 3 teaspoons milk. Add the dissolved soda to the cake batter. Add the mashed prunes. Coat two 8-inch round cake pans with vegetable spray and line the bottoms with wax paper. Fill the pans three-quarters full. Extra batter can be made into cupcakes or baked in a custard cup. Bake for 1¼ hours, or until a toothpick inserted in the cake comes out clean. Let the pans cool for 10 minutes. Before removing from pan to cake rack, frost with Seven-Minute Frosting (recipe follows).

Makes 8 servings

Seven-Minute Frosting

BRUCE KNECHTGES, SPECIAL EFFECTS

3 egg whites
2¼ cups sugar
1½ tablespoons light corn syrup
1 teaspoon vanilla extract

Combine the egg whites, sugar, corn syrup, and ½ cup water in the top of a double boiler. Over boiling water, beat constantly with an electric mixer until the icing is fluffy and holds its shape, about 7 minutes. Do not overcook, as it will become dry and chalky. Remove the icing and add the vanilla. Mix well and spread at once onto a cooled Prune Cake (preceding recipe) or cake of your choice.

Makes 2 cups: enough to frost one 9-inch layer cake

Rocky Road Cake

NANCY GOODMAN ILAND, FOODSTYLIST

2 cups semisweet chocolate chips
  or milk chocolate chips
4 large eggs, separated
¼ cup sugar
1 teaspoon vanilla extract
1 pint whipping cream, whipped
1 (10-inch) angel food cake
1 cup chopped walnuts or pecans

In the top of a double boiler, melt the chocolate chips, slowly adding the egg yolks and sugar until completely melted. Remove from heat. Add the vanilla. Beat the egg whites and fold in. Fold in the whipped cream. Tear the angel food cake into pieces and layer the bottom of a lightly greased tube pan. Add a layer of chocolate mixture, then a layer of nuts. Repeat, ending with the nuts. Chill overnight or freeze it and defrost for 1 hour. Serve at room temperature.

Makes 12 servings

Jessica's Cheesecake

ANGELA LANSBURY, ACTRESS

1½ cups graham cracker crumbs
¾ cup plus 2 tablespoons sugar
4 tablespoons butter or margarine, melted
11 ounces cream cheese, softened
2 large eggs, well beaten
1½ teaspoons vanilla extract
2 cups sour cream
2 teaspoons almond extract

Preheat the oven to 350°F. Combine the crumbs, 2 tablespoons sugar, and butter. Press into the bottom and sides of a 9-inch pie plate. Bake for exactly 5 minutes. Remove from the oven and let cool completely. Blend the cream cheese and half the beaten eggs thoroughly with an electric mixer. When blended, add the remaining eggs and mix thoroughly. Gradually add the vanilla and ½ cup of the sugar. Pour into the baked crust. Bake for 20 minutes. Mix the remaining ¼ cup sugar with the sour cream and almond extract. Spread over the cheesecake. Turn off the oven. Place the pie in the hot oven for exactly 4 minutes. Remove, chill, and serve.

Makes 6 to 8 servings

Super Rich Mint Brownies

KATHERINE WALLACE, EXECUTIVE ASSISTANT TO MS. LANSBURY

½ pound (2 sticks) butter, melted
1 cup sugar
6 large eggs
1 cup cocoa
1 teaspoon salt
2 cups flour
1 teaspoon vanilla extract

Preheat the oven to 350°F. Mix together the melted butter, sugar, and eggs. Sift in the cocoa, salt, and flour. Add the vanilla and beat well. Bake in a 9 by 13-inch pan for 30 minutes. Do not overcook. While the brownies cook, beat together the confectioners' sugar, softened butter, mint extract, and

2 cups confectioners' sugar
4 tablespoons butter, softened
2 teaspoons mint extract
2 teaspoons milk
8 ounces semisweet chocolate,
  melted

milk. Wait until the brownies have cooled to frost them, then chill in the refrigerator. When chilled, spread the melted semisweet chocolate on top. The flavor will intensify if stored in the refrigerator for a few days.

Makes 24 brownies

Canadian Buttertart Squares

KATHERINE WALLACE, EXECUTIVE ASSISTANT TO MS. LANSBURY

¼ pound (1 stick) margarine,
  softened
1 cup all-purpose flour
1½ cups plus 1 tablespoon light
  or dark brown sugar
2 large eggs
½ cup old-fashioned oats
½ cup chopped nuts (any type)
¼ teaspoon salt
½ teaspoon baking powder
1 teaspoon vanilla extract

*P*reheat the oven to 350°F. Cut together the margarine, flour, and 1 tablespoon brown sugar, or combine in food processor using the blade attachment. Press into a 9-inch square pan and bake for 15 minutes. Mix together the eggs, 1½ cups brown sugar, oats, nuts, salt, baking powder, and vanilla and pour over the partially baked crust. Bake 20 minutes. Cool and cut into squares.

Makes 12 squares

Fudge Brownies

EILEEN A. DUNN, COSTUMER

1 pound bittersweet chocolate, finely chopped
½ pound (2 sticks) unsalted butter, cut into tablespoons
⅓ cup strong brewed coffee
4 large eggs
1½ cups sugar
½ cup all-purpose flour
6 ounces walnut halves, coarsely chopped (about 2 cups)

Position a rack in the center of the oven, and preheat the oven to 375°F. Line a 9 by 13-inch baking pan with a double thickness of aluminum foil so that the foil extends 2 inches above the sides of the pan. Butter the bottom and sides of the foil-lined pan. In the top of a double boiler set over hot, not simmering, water, combine the chocolate, butter, and coffee, stirring frequently until smooth. Remove the pan from the heat. Cool the mixture, stirring occasionally, for 10 minutes. Set aside. In a large bowl, using a handheld mixer, beat the eggs for 30 seconds, or until foamy. Gradually add the sugar and continue to beat for 2 minutes, or until the mixture is very light and fluffy. Reduce the mixer speed to low and gradually beat in the chocolate mixture until just blended. Using a wooden spoon, stir in the flour. Stir in the walnuts. Do not overbeat. Transfer the batter to the prepared pan. Bake for 28 minutes to ½ hour. Cover the pan tightly with aluminum foil and chill for at least 6 hours or overnight. Remove the top foil and run a sharp knife around the edge. Using two ends of the foil as handles, invert the brownies onto a smooth surface and cut into rectangles.

Makes 16 brownies

Chocolate Chip Macaroons

BILL GREGORY, SET DECORATOR

⅓ cup flour
¼ teaspoon baking powder
⅛ teaspoon salt
¾ cup sugar
2 large eggs
1 tablespoon butter, melted
  and cooled
1 teaspoon vanilla extract
10 ounces shredded coconut
1 cup chocolate chips
1 cup semisweet chocolate bits,
  melted

*P*reheat the oven to 325°F. Sift together the flour, baking powder, and salt and set aside. With an electric mixer on high speed, cream the sugar and eggs for 5 minutes. Fold in the sifted flour mixture, butter, vanilla, coconut, and chocolate chips. Drop by rounded teaspoonful onto foil-lined cookie sheets. Bake for 18 minutes, reversing the sheets top to bottom and front to back once during baking. Spread the melted semisweet chocolate on cooled cookie bottoms. Place on foil-lined cookie sheets until set. Store in an airtight container at room temperature.

Makes 36 cookies

Oatmeal Cookies

CHRIS BATEMAN, ELECTRICIAN

1 cup vegetable shortening
½ cup dark brown sugar
3 large eggs
½ cup buttermilk
1¾ cups flour
1 teaspoon baking soda
1 tablespoon baking powder
1 teaspoon salt
1 teaspoon ground cinnamon
1 teaspoon ground nutmeg
3 cups quick-cooking oats
1 cup raisins
½ cup chopped walnuts (optional)

Preheat the oven to 400°F. Mix the shortening, brown sugar, and eggs together until light and fluffy. Stir in the buttermilk. In a separate bowl, mix together the flour, baking soda, baking powder, salt, cinnamon, and nutmeg. Blend thoroughly and combine with the shortening mixture. Add the oats, raisins, nuts if using, and mix. Spoon onto a lightly greased cookie sheet, about 3 inches apart. For chewier cookies, add ½ cup coconut with the raisins and nuts. Bake for 10 to 12 minutes.

Makes 4 dozen cookies

Lemon Cheese Topping

BILL BROCHTRUP, ACTOR

¼ pound (1 stick) butter
2 cups sugar
4 large eggs, beaten
¾ cup lemon juice

In the top of a double boiler, melt the butter over hot water. Remove from heat and place in a mixing bowl. Add 1 cup of the sugar, then slowly add the beaten eggs, then the remainder of the sugar, then the lemon juice. Transfer back to the double boiler and cook over low heat, stirring constantly, until it reaches a puddinglike consistency. Chill. Serve over scones or biscuits.

Makes 2 cups

Graham Dream Bars

ZANNE SHAW, STAND-IN TO MS. LANSBURY

10 graham cracker squares
½ cup packed light or dark
  brown sugar
1 tablespoon cornstarch
¼ teaspoon salt
¼ pound (1 stick) butter,
  cut into tablespoons
½ cup confectioners' sugar
1 cup flaked coconut
½ cup chopped pecans
1 cup semisweet chocolate pieces

*A*rrange the cracker squares to cover the bottom of a 12 by 9-inch microwave dish, cutting to fit as necessary. Set aside. Combine the brown sugar, cornstarch, and salt in a 1-quart microwave safe casserole dish or bowl, blending well. Cut in the butter. Microwave on HIGH for 2 to 3 minutes, stirring to blend every 30 seconds until the mixture is smooth and slightly thickened. Stir in the confectioners' sugar, coconut, and nuts and quickly spread over the crackers. Sprinkle the chocolate pieces evenly over the coconut layer and return to microwave on MEDIUM for 3 to 4 minutes, just until the chips appear shiny in most areas. With a small spatula or knife, spread the chocolate evenly over the tops of the cookies. Cut into small squares and cool.

Makes 26 bars

Butterscotch Haystack Cookies

FRANZ PLETH, MOTOR HOME DRIVER TO MS. LANSBURY

8 ounces butterscotch chips
4 tablespoons butter or margarine
¾ cup peanut butter
8 ounces chow mein noodles

*M*elt the butterscotch chips, butter, and peanut butter in the top of a double boiler. When melted, pour in the noodles and coat completely. Drop onto wax paper. Let set until hard.

Makes 3 dozen cookies

Hint D'Mint Drops

FRANZ PLETH, MOTOR HOME DRIVER TO MS. LANSBURY

*12 tablespoons (1½ sticks) butter
or margarine, softened*

½ cup sugar

*1 cup packed light or dark brown
sugar*

1 large egg

1 teaspoon vanilla extract

*2½ cups quick-cooking or old-
fashioned oats*

1¼ cups flour

½ teaspoon salt

½ teaspoon baking soda

1 cup semisweet chocolate bits

*⅓ cup finely crushed peppermint
candy (about 6 candy canes)*

Preheat the oven to 350°F. Beat together the butter, sugar, and brown sugar until light and fluffy. Blend in the egg, 1 tablespoon water, and vanilla. Add the oats, flour, salt, and baking soda. Mix well. Stir in the chocolate bits and peppermint candy. Drop by tablespoons onto an ungreased cookie sheet, spaced 2 inches apart. Bake for 12 to 14 minutes, or until golden brown. Cool for 1 minute on the cookie sheet, then transfer to a wire rack and let cool completely.

Makes 3 dozen cookies

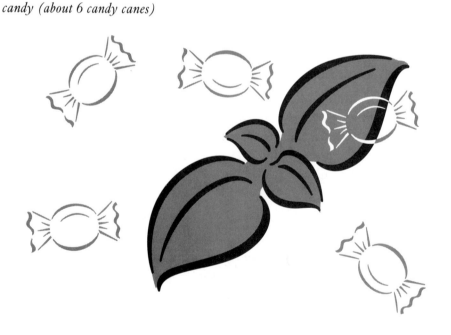

Kaye's Kabot Kove Kookies

RON MASAK, ACTOR

¼ pound (1 stick) butter
1½ cups graham cracker crumbs
1 cup semisweet chocolate chips
1 cup butterscotch chips
1½ cups grated coconut
1½ cups chopped nuts (any type)
1 can (14 ounces) Eagle Brand
  sweetened condensed milk

*P*reheat the oven to 350°F. Melt the butter in a 9 by 13-inch pan. Sprinkle the crumbs over the butter. Add the chocolate chips, butterscotch chips, coconut, and nuts. Press down with hands. Pour the condensed milk over all. Bake for 25 minutes to ½ hour or until lightly browned. Let cool. Do not cut while hot. Cut into squares and serve.

Makes 1 dozen cookies

Lemon Bars

BILL PURVIANCE, DRIVER

½ pound (2 sticks) margarine,
  melted
2 cups plus 4 tablespoons flour
½ cup confectioners' sugar
4 large eggs
1¼ cups sugar
6 tablespoons fresh lemon juice
½ teaspoon baking powder

*P*reheat the oven to 350°F. Combine the margarine, 2 cups flour, and confectioners' sugar. Press into a 9 by 13-inch ungreased pan. Bake for 10 to 12 minutes, or until golden brown. Meanwhile, in a mixing bowl, beat together the eggs, sugar, and lemon juice until thickened. Sift together 4 tablespoons flour and baking powder and add to the eggs. Blend. Pour over the crust. Bake for 20 to 25 minutes. Sprinkle extra confectioners' sugar over the top, if desired. Slice into bars to serve.

Makes 16 bars

Chocolate Coconut Bars

JOELLEN WALLER, ACTRESS

6 tablespoons butter, melted
1½ cups graham cracker crumbs
2 cups toasted coconut
2 cups chocolate chips
2 cups almonds, walnuts, or pecans
1 can (14 ounces) Eagle Brand
 sweetened condensed milk

*P*reheat the oven to 350°F. Coat a 9 by 13-inch cookie sheet with the melted butter. Layer the graham cracker crumbs, coconut, chocolate chips, and nuts. Slowly pour the condensed milk over the mixture, covering it all. Bake for 25 minutes. Slice into bars and serve.

Makes 18 bars

Molasses Crinkies

KELLY CANTLEY, SECOND ASSISTANT DIRECTOR

1 cup packed light or dark
 brown sugar
¼ pound (1 stick) butter or
 margarine, softened
¼ cup vegetable shortening
¼ cup molasses
1 large egg
2 cups all-purpose flour
2 teaspoons baking soda
1 teaspoon ground cinnamon
1 teaspoon ground ginger
½ teaspoon ground cloves
¼ teaspoon salt
1 cup sugar

*M*ix together the brown sugar, butter, shortening, molasses, and egg in a medium bowl. Stir in the remaining ingredients except sugar. Cover and chill for at least 1 hour but no more than 24 hours. Preheat the oven to 375°F. Shape the dough into 1¼-inch balls and roll in the sugar. Place about 2 inches apart on ungreased cookie sheets. Bake for 10 to 11 minutes, or until set. Cool slightly, then remove from cookie sheets.

Makes 3 dozen cookies

Peanut Butter Bars

OFFICER CLARK, LOCATION POLICE

2 cups peanut butter
½ cup plus 1 tablespoon melted
butter
2¾ cups confectioners' sugar
12 ounces chocolate chips

*S*tir together the peanut butter, ½ cup of the melted butter, and confectioners' sugar. Press the mixture into the bottom of a 9-inch square pan. Melt the chocolate chips and stir together with the remaining tablespoon of melted butter: spread on top. Chill in the refrigerator for 10 minutes before cutting. Store at room temperature.

Makes 12 bars

Vanilla Ice Cream

ANN DAVIES, SECRETARY TO MS. LANSBURY

½ cup sugar
⅛ teaspoon salt
4 to 6 egg yolks, beaten
2 cups scalded milk
1 pint heavy cream
1 teaspoon vanilla extract

*M*ix together the sugar, salt, and egg yolks in the top of a double boiler. Pour in the milk, stirring constantly. Cook until the mixture coats the spoon. Cool, then strain. Add the cream and vanilla and freeze in an ice cream freezer. For a variation, mix in chocolate chips, cookie crumbles, fruit, or candy pieces when you add the cream.

Makes 8 servings

Hot Fudge Sauce

KATHERINE WALLACE, EXECUTIVE ASSISTANT TO MS. LANSBURY

8 tablespoons cornstarch
2 cups milk
2 cups sugar
4 tablespoons cocoa
½ teaspoon salt
½ teaspoon vanilla extract
4 tablespoons butter

*I*n a saucepan, mix together the cornstarch and milk. Add the sugar, cocoa, and salt. Heat over medium heat, stirring constantly. When thick, remove from heat and add the vanilla and butter. Serve over ice cream.

Makes 2 cups

Caramel Candy

LISA WILCOX, ACTRESS

2 cups sugar
1 cup light Karo syrup
12 ounces evaporated milk
½ cup (1 stick) butter or margarine

*I*n a deep pot, mix together all the ingredients. Cook and stir constantly to 238°F (you need a candy thermometer). When you reach 238°F, pour into a greased 8-inch square metal pan. Chill until firm or overnight. Remove and let the candy get soft enough to cut into 1-inch cubes. Wrap in 5 by 5-inch pieces of wax paper.

Makes 1½ pounds

World's Best Fudge

PAUL CONTI, COMPUTER GRAPHICS

¼ pound (1 stick) butter, melted
2 cups walnut or pecan pieces
1 teaspoon vanilla extract
2 cups chocolate chips
2 cups sugar
11 large marshmallows
1 can (5 ounces) evaporated milk

Mix together the butter, nuts, vanilla, and chocolate chips in a large bowl and set aside. In a large saucepan, bring the sugar, marshmallows, and evaporated milk to a boil for 6 minutes, stirring constantly with a wooden spoon to avoid scorching. Pour the hot mixture over the butter mixture and beat well with a wooden spoon, then pour into a greased pan. Let cool and cut into squares.

Makes 1½ pounds

Chocolate Fudge

ERIC WOODALL, ACTOR

3 cups sugar
3 heaping tablespoons cocoa
1½ tablespoons light Karo syrup
1½ cups milk
¼ pound (1 stick) butter, softened
1 cup walnut pieces (optional)

Mix together all ingredients except the butter and nuts. Cook until it reaches 250°F on a candy thermometer, or until a soft ball forms when a bit of the mixture is dropped into a glass of water. Remove from the stove, add the butter and nuts, and let cool to room temperature. Then beat by hand and drop onto wax paper by spoonfuls.

Makes 2 pounds

Peanut Butter Fudge

FRANK MCNAIR, SECURITY GUARD

2 cups sugar
3 tablespoons butter
1 cup evaporated milk
1 cup miniature marshmallows
12 ounces peanut butter
1 teaspoon vanilla extract

*M*ix together the sugar, butter, and evaporated milk in a skillet. Boil for 5 minutes. Turn off heat. Add the marshmallows, peanut butter, and vanilla. Mix until the marshmallows are completely melted. Pour into a buttered 9-inch square pan. Let cool, then cut into squares.

Makes 1 pound

Chocolate Truffles

LON MASSEY, CHIEF LIGHTING TECHNICIAN

1 cup heavy cream
2 pounds bittersweet chocolate,
 finely chopped
3 tablespoons unsalted butter

*I*n a heavy pan, bring the cream to a simmer (a microwave and a glass bowl is just as good for this). Remove from the heat and whisk in 10 ounces, about 1½ cups, of the chocolate and the butter. Chill for 4 hours, until firmly set, stirring occasionally. If you cool this in the freezer, freeze for 1 hour and stir frequently. Using a melon baller or spoon, scoop out 1 tablespoon or so of the chilled mixture and use your hands to form balls about ¾ inch to 1 inch in diameter. Place them on a cookie sheet and freeze for 1 hour. While the balls are freezing, carefully heat the remaining chocolate in the top of a double boiler or heavy pot. Stir until melted. Allow to slowly cool until it feels just warm to the touch. The object is to have the chocolate just above the melting point so that when the frozen chocolate balls are dipped in it, they gather a thickish coating around them. When the centers are frozen and the chocolate is ready, take each one and drop it into the coating, roll it quickly about, then remove it with the tines of two forks and drop it onto a sheet of wax paper. If the coating thickens too much, reheat it a little in the pot or microwave. When all the truffles are dipped, you can serve them right away. If they are to be stored or transported, chill them first. As a variation, add 6 ounces chopped blanched almonds to the truffle mixture when it is lukewarm but not yet set, then proceed as before. You can also sprinkle the almonds over the truffles just after dipping.

Makes 30 truffles

ELEVEN

Breakfasts

"Five years on the show and I never got to meet my TV wife. All those phone calls I made and received and there was no one on the other end. It was all imaginary. I would just think of my own beautiful wife and kids and then the calls were easy to make."

—*Ron Masak, actor*

Sunday Brunch Pancakes

JO DAVIS, WARDROBE

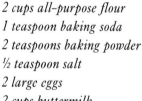

½ tablespoon butter
2 large eggs
½ cup flour
½ cup milk
Lemon juice to taste
Confectioners' sugar to taste

Preheat the oven to 425°F. Melt the butter in a shallow skillet. Beat the eggs in a separate bowl. Add the flour and milk and blend, but leave slightly lumpy. Pour the mixture into the hot skillet and cook until lightly browned on bottom. Place the skillet in the oven and bake for 15 minutes. When the pancake is fully cooked, remove to a plate, sprinkle with lemon juice and confectioners' sugar and top with fruit, jam, jelly, or syrup.

Makes 4 servings

Buttermilk Pancakes

SUZANNE WAITE, SCRIPT SUPERVISOR

2 cups all-purpose flour
1 teaspoon baking soda
2 teaspoons baking powder
½ teaspoon salt
2 large eggs
2 cups buttermilk
2 tablespoons vegetable oil
Butter or oil for frying

Sift the flour, baking soda, baking powder, and salt together and set aside. In a large bowl, beat the eggs with the buttermilk and 2 tablespoons oil. Add the flour mixture and stir. Pour the pancake batter by spoonfuls onto a hot greased griddle or skillet. When bubbles emerge and the edges begin to look dry, flip the pancakes. Do not overflip as this makes them tough. Keep cooked pancakes in a warmed oven until ready to serve.

Makes 6 servings

Oatmeal Pancakes

ZANNE SHAW, STAND-IN TO MS. LANSBURY

1 cup old-fashioned oats
1 cup buttermilk
1 large egg
½ teaspoon baking soda
1 tablespoon butter, melted
Butter or oil for frying

*I*n a large bowl mix together the oats and buttermilk and let soak for ½ hour. Add egg, baking soda, and butter and mix. If batter is too thick then add a little water. Pour batter onto a hot greased griddle or skillet. These are great served with preserves, maple syrup, or marmalade.

Makes 2 servings

Breakfast Oatcakes

TIME WINTERS, ACTOR

1½ cups rolled oats
¼ pound (1 stick) butter or mar-
  garine (may substitute ½ cup
  canola oil or a mixture)
1 large egg
Sea salt to taste

*I*n a hot skillet, dry roast the rolled oats until they have a nice nutty aroma. Add the butter and coat the oats thoroughly. Remove from heat. Add the egg and salt and mix well. Press the mixture into the bottom of the skillet and heat until the edges bubble. Cover the pan with a large plate and flip the pan over, slide the oatcake back into the pan and heat other side. The oatcake should be golden brown. Remove from heat. Serve hot, whole or cut in half, with maple syrup or puréed fruit heated with a touch of molasses. The oatcakes can be served hot in winter or cold in summer.

Makes 2 oatcakes

French Toast

KELLY CANTLEY, SECOND ASSISTANT DIRECTOR

4 large eggs, beaten
½ cup milk
1 teaspoon vanilla extract
Ground cinnamon to taste
1 loaf French bread (can be a
*   day old or older), cut into 1-inch*
*   slices*
1 tablespoon butter

Combine the eggs, milk, vanilla, and cinnamon in a bowl. Dip both sides of French bread slices into the egg mixture quickly. Do not let it soak. Melt the butter in a large skillet and fry the bread over medium heat until both sides are golden brown. Serve immediately with confectioners' sugar and orange marmalade or maple syrup.

Makes 6 servings

Crackers and Eggs

LEE POLL, SET DECORATOR

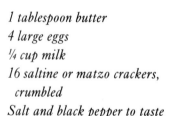

1 tablespoon butter
4 large eggs
¼ cup milk
16 saltine or matzo crackers,
*   crumbled*
Salt and black pepper to taste

Melt the butter in a medium skillet. In a small bowl, scramble together the eggs and milk. Then add the crackers, salt, and pepper. Pour into a skillet and cook to desired doneness. Serve immediately.

Makes 2 servings

Poor Man's Breakfast

TOM CULVER, WARDROBE

4 small Irish potatoes
2 tablespoons butter
1 cup sliced fresh mushrooms
2 cloves garlic, minced
2 large eggs, beaten
2 tablespoons milk

*B*oil the potatoes in their skins. Drain and slice thin. Sauté the potatoes in the butter for about 5 minutes, adding the mushrooms and garlic during the last 2 minutes. Mix the eggs and milk together in a separate bowl and pour over the potatoes. Cook over medium heat, stirring often, until the eggs are firm. Serve with coffee and wheat toast with marmalade.

Makes 2 servings

Brother Juniper Breakfast

ALLAN MILLER, ACTOR

½ package (8 ounces) firm tofu,
  cut into ⅛-inch thick slices
¼ cup soy sauce
1 medium potato
2 teaspoons olive oil
1 green bell pepper, chopped
2 scallions, chopped
½ pound mushrooms, chopped
1 medium tomato, sliced
2 bagels or English muffins

*I*n a small bowl, combine the tofu and soy sauce. Microwave the potato for 3 minutes, then cut into slices and add to the bowl. Sauté the marinated tofu and potato slices in the olive oil until browned. Add the green pepper, scallions, mushrooms, and tomato and cook until warmed through. Toast the bagels or the English muffins. Serve alongside or over the toast.

Makes 2 servings

Easy Texas Hash

GERALD S. O'LOUGHLIN, ACTOR

1 pound ground beef
2 or 3 large yellow onions, sliced
1 large green bell pepper, chopped
1 can (1 pound, 28 ounces)
  crushed tomatoes
½ cup uncooked white rice
1 teaspoon chili powder
1½ teaspoons salt
1 teaspoon black pepper

*P*reheat the oven to 350°F. In a large skillet, cook and stir the ground beef until light brown: drain off fat. Add the onions and green pepper and cook, stirring until the onions are tender. Stir in the tomatoes, rice, chili powder, salt, and pepper and cook until heated through. Pour into an ungreased 2-quart casserole dish. Cover and bake for 1 hour. Serve hot.

Makes 4 servings

Mexican Scramble

DON VARGAS, KEY WARDROBE

6 large eggs, beaten with a splash
  of milk
1 cup crushed tortilla chips
½ cup shredded Monterey Jack
  cheese
2 scallions, chopped, including
  some green

*I*n a bowl, blend all the ingredients together by hand. Cook over medium heat in a buttered nonstick skillet until the eggs are firm. Serve with salsa and sourdough toast.

Makes 2 servings

Monte Cristo Breakfast Sandwich

NANCY GOODMAN ILAND, FOODSTYLIST

2 large eggs, well beaten
1½ tablespoons heavy cream
Salt to taste
2 thin slices cold turkey or chicken breast
2 thin slices ham
2 slices Monterey Jack or Swiss cheese
2 slices white bread
1 tablespoon butter or margerine

In a shallow bowl, mix together the eggs, cream, and salt. Place the meats and cheese slices between slices of bread. Cut sandwich in half and quickly dip in egg mixture. Sauté the sandwich halves in the butter or margarine until golden brown on each side. Serve with strawberry jam.

Makes 1 serving

Overnight Breakfast Casserole

FRANK MCNAIR, SECURITY GUARD

1 pound bulk sausage, crumbled
6 large eggs, beaten
2 cups milk
1 teaspoon dry mustard
1 teaspoon salt
6 slices bread, trimmed and cubed
1 cup shredded Cheddar cheese
1 can (8 ounces) sliced mushrooms (optional)

In a skillet over medium heat, cook the sausage, drain, and set aside. In a large bowl, beat together the eggs, milk, dry mustard, and salt. Add the bread cubes, cheese, reserved sausage, and mushrooms if using. Pour into a 3-quart greased baking dish and chill overnight. Preheat the oven to 350°F. Bake, covered, at for 45 minutes. Uncover during the last 10 minutes. Serve hot.

Makes 6 servings

Sgt. Boyle's Red-Eye Eggs Benedict

MARK ROLSTON, ACTOR

1½ to 2 pounds country-smoked ham steaks
2 tablespoons butter
½ cup cold coffee
8 large biscuits, halved
6 tablespoons white wine vinegar
1 teaspoon ground white pepper
3 tablespoons fresh lemon juice
3 egg yolks
12 tablespoons (1½ sticks) butter, melted
8 large eggs
6 jalapeño peppers, halved

Fry the ham steaks in a large skillet. Remove from the pan, trim into rounds, and set aside. Add the butter and coffee to the grease left in the pan, reduce for a few minutes over medium heat, and set aside. This will be the red-eye gravy that gives this dish its unique flavor.

Toast the biscuit halves and set aside. In a deep skillet, boil enough water to poach the eggs, adding 3 tablespoons of the vinegar to assist poaching. While the water boils, make the hollandaise sauce: in a medium saucepan, boil ¾ cup water with the white pepper, the remaining 3 tablespoons vinegar, and the lemon juice. When the liquid is reduced to just covering the pan, add 3 tablespoons cold water and the egg yolks, whisking continually so as not to cook the yolks. Remove the saucepan from the heat completely if necessary: the sauce can scramble quickly. As soon as the yolks froth up, start adding the melted butter, whisking continually, until a thick sauce is formed. Add 3 tablespoons of the reserved red-eye gravy.

Poach the eggs in the boiling water and vinegar, removing them when done with a slotted spoon. Set the biscuits side by side on serving plates. Layer the ham rounds onto the biscuits, then the eggs. Cover in hollandaise sauce and garnish each with a jalapeño half. Home-cooked potatoes with paprika are a good complement to this dish, as are grilled tomatoes or asparagus.

Makes 4 servings

TWELVE

Beverages

"I was a main character on **Murder, She Wrote** for five years, playing Andy, the deputy sheriff, and I never developed an on-screen relationship with anyone other than the sheriff. Then one day during the show's last season, one of the producers came up to me in the hall and told me that they were going to feature me in an upcoming episode. I was delighted. Finally, I got to wear street clothes and get the girl, and to top it off, I was an actual suspect in a murder case. Wow, what fun, a real turnaround for my character and a great way to end the show for me."

—Louis Herthum, actor

Irish Cream Liqueur

OFFICER CLARK, LOCATION POLICE

1 can (14 ounces) Eagle Brand
  condensed milk
2 tablespoons chocolate syrup
1 teaspoon vanilla extract
1 teaspoon coconut oil
3 eggs
6 to 8 ounces blended bourbon

*M*ix all the ingredients together in a blender for 10 to 20 seconds. Serve as is or with ice.

Makes 8 servings

Holiday Wassail

ROBERT PINE, ACTOR

1 tablespoon whole cloves
1 tablespoon whole allspice
1 cup packed dark brown sugar
1 gallon apple cider
6 ounces frozen lemonade
6 ounces frozen orange juice
1 teaspoon ground nutmeg
12 cinnamon sticks
½ to 1 ounce dark rum per serving
  (optional)

*T*ie the cloves and allspice in a cheesecloth bag. This can be left in the wassail even while serving. In a bowl, mix the brown sugar and enough cider to completely dissolve the sugar. In a 6-quart kettle, combine the cheesecloth bag of spices, the dissolved sugar, cider, frozen lemonade, frozen orange juice, nutmeg, and cinnamon. Stir to mix thoroughly and simmer for 20 minutes. Stir occasionally. Do not boil. Add rum as desired to the serving glasses, and fill with wassail. This is delicious with or without rum and perfect for the holiday season.

Makes 18 to 24 servings

Authentic Swedish Glögg

SHANNON LITTEN, KEY WARDROBE

1 cup blanched almonds
1 cup seedless raisins
¾ pound pitted prunes
¼ peel of 1 orange
15 whole cloves
2 sticks cinnamon
2 ounces fresh peeled ginger root
12 cardamom pods
1 gallon port wine
⅘ quart brandy, plus extra for soaking
⅘ quart aquavit (Aalborg), plus extra for soaking
1 pint dark rum
¾ cup sugar (optional)

Combine ½ cup of the almonds, all but ½ cup of the raisins, the prunes, orange peel, cloves, cinnamon, ginger, cardamom, and 1 quart water in a large saucepan. Cover and simmer for 45 minutes. Pour into a large kettle. Add port. Cover tightly and heat to just below boiling point, then turn off heat. Carefully add the brandy, aquavit, and rum. Cover and carefully heat again to just below boiling point. Do not boil. Turn off heat and let cool, covered, about 5 minutes. Remove the cover. Light a match and carefully light the surface of the wine mixture. Let burn 1 to 2 seconds. Quickly cover tightly to smother the flame. Light again and let burn for another 1 to 2 seconds. Cover to smother flame again. Add the sugar if using. Soak the remaining ½ cup almonds and ½ cup raisins in a little aquavit or brandy overnight, then place in the bottom of the serving cups. Heat to just below boiling before serving.

Makes 22 (6-ounce) servings

243

Jamaican-Sorrel Christmas Drink

GENEVA NASH-MORGAN, MAKEUP

3-inch piece fresh ginger, peeled
  and chopped
1 teaspoon ground nutmeg
3 cinnamon sticks
5 cups jamica (dried red hibiscus
  flowers, available from specialty
  stores)
4 cups light or dark brown sugar

*F*ill an 8-quart pan with water up to 3 inches from the top. Add the ginger, nutmeg, and cinnamon sticks and bring to a boil. Turn off the heat and add the jamica. Cover and let it steep overnight on the stove with no heat on. Add the brown sugar. Stir and taste. If too tart, add another 1 to 2 cups sugar. Stir. Strain the liquid into containers, cover, and refrigerate. Serve over ice.

Makes 24 servings

Homemade Kahlúa

OFFICER CLARK, LOCATION POLICE

4 cups white or brown sugar
4 cups boiling water
1 jar (2 ounces) instant Yuban
  coffee (may substitute any high-
  quality instant coffee)
4 cups 100-proof vodka
3 tablespoons vanilla extract

*M*ix together the sugar, water, and coffee in a large pan. Boil for 1 minute. Let cool. Add the vodka and vanilla. Pour into bottles and let stand overnight.

Makes 10 servings

Behind the Scenes. . . Who Does What

Actors These are the people working in front of the camera on screen. Actors and actresses do just that. The stuntmen and stunt doubles step in to act out the dangerous scenes, like Angela hitting the ground to dodge a bullet, or a fight scene. Atmosphere refers to silent actors called "extras" used to fill in the background of a crowded street or restaurant scene. Stand-ins are actors who take the place of the cast members during the setup of lighting and camera angles. They also read lines for actors who may not be present during the shooting of a scene.

Art Director Working closely with the production designer, the art director oversees the art department and coordinates the sets and selects the signage and all other visual elements of the sets.

Atmosphere See Actors.

Best Boy See Set Lighting.

Boom Man See Sound.

Camera This department includes the first assistant camera, second assistant camera, and all the camera operators. They are responsible for anything that has to do with operating the camera itself. This includes getting film and maintaining the cameras. *Murder, She Wrote* generally used one or two cameras for shooting. The head of this department is the director of photography.

Carpenter See Set Dressers.

Computer Graphics When a computer screen appears on film either in the background to add realism, or on display to convey a specific message or image, the computer graphics person sets that up.

Construction See Set Dressers.

Costumers Key costumers shop for and fit all the actors. Set costumers maintain all the accessories, put the wardrobe in the actors' dressing rooms, and keep a continuity book with photos of every costume change. As most television shows and films are shot out of time sequence, this job becomes very important. This department includes supervisors, key costumers, and set costumers.

Craft Services They provide snacks for the hungry actors and crew on the set throughout the day. They also keep the set clean and are allowed by the union to help out when anything needs to be moved or operated on the set.

Director Working closely with the producers, the director takes the actors through each scene. *Murder, She Wrote* throughout the years used different directors for different episodes. The director OKs virtually everything concerning the movie or television show.

Director of Photography Working closely with the director, the director of photography directs the cameramen where to shoot, from what directions, and from what angles. The director of photography ensures that everything that is seen through the camera appears just right.

Dolly Grip See Grips.

Electrician See Set Lighting.

Estimator This is the person who works out the budget for the show and lets the producers and directors know whether or not they can afford to film on location in Paris or on the back lot.

First Assistant Director Next in line after the director, the first assistant director keeps the show moving and prepares a schedule of the entire movie or episode. This person is typically a cross between a second-grade teacher and a traffic cop.

Foodstylist The foodstylist designs and displays all the food that will be seen on the show. This includes anything the actors will be eating at a party, in a restaurant, or in their kitchen.

Gaffer See Set Lighting.

Grips Grips work directly with the cameraman and gaffer to light and shoot a scene. The responsibilities of the dolly grip include camera movement using cranes and dollies. The other grips assist with lighting by the use of scrims and flags; taking apart and putting together the set while filming; and numerous other duties.

Lighting Technicians See Set Lighting.

Location Manager When off the set and on location, the location manager is responsible for taking care of everything at that site. This person's responsibilities include ensuring that nothing on location gets damaged or ruined during the filming and scouts the location in order to know how to get in and out and where to park.

Location Police and Security They keep the set safe for the actors and crew and keep unauthorized personnel off the set. They also control the traffic flow when shooting.

Makeup Artists and Hairstylists Each actor is assigned a makeup artist and hairstylist who works with them to maintain the look of the show. Makeup artists and hairstylists work closely with wardrobe. There is always a makeup artist and a hairstylist on the set while shooting to retouch the actors', hair and makeup and generally maintain the continuity of their appearance throughout the episode.

Producers Executive producers, associate producers, supervising producers, coproducers, and assistant producers all oversee the project from concept to delivery. They rule the show.

Production Assistants They are in training to climb the director's ladder and do a variety of tasks that support the entire production.

Production Coordinator The production coordinator brings together everything for the show in order to take care of the cast and crew. This person is ground zero for the whole show, meaning everything from paychecks to script revisions.

Production Designer The production designer oversees the entire look of the show and coordinates the style and colors of the set, the wardrobe, makeup, and hair. This person works closely with the producers and art director.

Prop Master The prop master is in charge of the prop department. The prop department deals with anything that the actors handle during the shoot, such as cigarettes, food, drinks, guns, papers, and pencils—anything that is not nailed down. The set prop persons are on the set during the entire shooting process and they take over where the set dressers leave off. Working closely with the production designers and their department, the prop master also picks out special pieces the actors will work with. The bigger the production, the larger the crew and the more props. Directly under the prop master are usually two or three propmen or women who move furniture and give actors their props, be it guns, watches, or name tags.

Script Supervisor Working closely with the director to maintain continuity throughout the entire movie or television episode, the script supervisor carries a book to keep track of everything that is shot and what is needed for the next scene. This person is also responsible for checking all the dialogue and always knows which shoulder the purse was on. This job is details, details, details.

Second Assistant Director Next in charge after the first assistant director, the second assistant director knows everything that's going on with the show. Usually extremely busy, this person handles the extras, informs the actors of the daily scheduling, and makes sure they are ready for their next scene and are on the set. If you ever need anything on the set you can always ask the second assistant director.

Set Decorator With guidance from the production designer, this person shops for furniture, drapery, wallpaper, lighting fixtures, and props.

Set Designer The set designer is a draftsman who designs the set on paper.

Set Dressers They do the actual work of putting furniture, pictures, rugs, and all other fixed props in place on the set. Carpenters, construction, and set painters are part of this department. They build the sets and paint the walls and work closely with the set decorator. The chief set dresser is the leadman.

Set Lighting A gaffer—the chief lighting technician—assists the director of photography in lighting the set and is responsible for the people and equipment to carry this out. The best boy is second in charge after the gaffer. The gaffer's crew includes lighting technicians and electricians who adjust and move around all the lights used on the set. They light night for day and day for night and make sure the light is just right for the actors.

Set Painter See Set Dresser.

Sound The sound mixer records the sounds and dialogue for the show. The utility sound technician assists the sound mixer. Sound and video playback repeats any sounds or video images played in the scene. The boom man operates the long booms holding the microphones above the actors' heads and out of view of the cameras. Other sound people put body microphones on the actors.

Sound Mixer See Sound.

Sound Playback See Sound.

Special Effects The people in this department are masters at creating atmosphere—rain, soft breezes, wind, fire, explosions, simulated bullet hits, and fog. They also set up any mechanical rigging needed for the story line, like elevators or blinking lights.

Stand-Ins See Actors.

Stuntmen See Actors.

Transportation The transportation captain, co-captains, and drivers are the real movers in the business. Anything that moves to and from or around the lot or on a location is their territory. They are typically the first on the set and the last to leave.

Utility Sound Technician See Sound.

Video Playback See Sound.

Wardrobe See Costumers.

THAT'S A WRAP!

Index

Red Peppers in Oil, 157
Russian Hot Cabbage Soup, 30
Ruth's Spinach Dip, 19
Salmon and Asparagus Fettucine with Basil Sauce, 128
Scalloped Corn and Tomatoes, 166
Scalloped Potatoes with Cheese, 154-55
Seafood Gazpacho, 33
Sopa de Albondigas, 24
South African Yogurt and Chicken Potjie, 88
Spanakopitta (Spinach Pie), 159
Spicy Black Beans, 121
Spinach Balls, 8-9
Spinach Pie, 160
Spinach-Stuffed Mushrooms, 9
Squash Casserole, 117
Stuffed Eggplant, 150-51
Stuffed Mushrooms, 8
Stuffed Zucchini, 164-65
Ten Bean Soup, 28
Tuscan Vegetable Bean Soup, 28-29
Twice-Baked Potatoes, 153
Val's Homemade Chicken Soup, 25

Veal with Artichokes and Linguine, 136-37
Vegetable Chili, 122
Vegetable Fritatta, 162
Vegetarian Lasagna, 137
Vegetarian Meat Loaf, 69
Warm New Red Potatoes with Rosemary, 158
Zucchini with Bacon, 165
See also specific kinds
Vercelli, Susan, 37, 72
Vesper, Eric, 59
Villarreal, Melinda, 197
Vodka Pasta, 138

W

Waite, Suzanne, 77, 89, 92, 171, 190, 234
Waldman, Sharon, 195, 210
Walker, Maggi, 108
Wallace, Katherine, 68, 186, 218, 219, 228
Waller, Joellen, 226
Walter, Jessica, 44, 187
Warm Francesca Salad, 46
Warm New Red Potatoes with Rosemary, 158
Warren, Jennifer, 2
Weis, James R., 20, 84, 121
Weist, Lucinda, 62
White, Brad, 51
White Chocolate Mousse with Fresh Raspberry Sauce, 203

White, Jeff, 136, 141
Whitehead, Dean, 126, 133
Wilcox, Lisa, 228
Wild Rice and Sausage Stuffing, 144
Williams, Bob, 2, 21
Windom, William, 139
Windom's Last Meal (Caviar and Grits), 139
Winters, Time, 235
Woodall, Eric, 205, 206, 229
World's Best Fudge, 229

Y

Yapraks (Grape Leaves Stuffed with Meat and Rice), 163
Yates, Cassie, 95
Yñiguez, Richard, 58
Yurtchuk, Vera, 30, 34, 143

Z

Zada, Ramy, 78, 155, 161
Zavala, Mario, 14
Zimmerman, George, 193
Zingy Clam Dip, 18
Zucchini
  Baked Zucchini, 164
  Ratatouille, 156-57
  Stuffed Zucchini, 164-65
  Zucchini with Bacon, 165
  Zucchini Bread, 182